**TRANSFER PRICING
PRACTICES** IN
THE **UNITED STATES**
AND **JAPAN**

ROGER Y. W. TANG

TRANSFER PRICING PRACTICES IN THE UNITED STATES AND JAPAN

PRAEGER PUBLISHERS
Praeger Special Studies

New York • London • Sydney • Toronto

Library of Congress Cataloging in Publication Data

Tang, Roger Y   W
    Transfer pricing in the United States and Japan.

    Bibliography: p.
    Includes index.
    1. Transfer pricing. 2. Price policy--Japan.
3. Price policy--United States. I. Title.
HF5416.5.T36   338.5'22'0952   78-19780
ISBN 0-03-046551-6

PRAEGER PUBLISHERS
PRAEGER SPECIAL STUDIES
383 Madison Avenue, New York, N.Y. 10017, U.S.A.

Published in the United States of America in 1979
by Praeger Publishers,
A Division of Holt, Rinehart and Winston, CBS, Inc.

9   038   987654321

Printed in the United States of America

PREFACE

Transfer pricing is one of the most pressing problems confronting corporate management of divisionalized firms. It is vital to company profits and to the evaluation of divisional performances. The issues on transfer pricing have also been discussed extensively in business literature for more than two decades. Most of the prior studies, however, deal with the theoretical merits of various pricing proposals or the domestic dimension of transfer pricing. Thus, many problems in this area remain unsolved today.

This book deals with the multinational as well as the domestic dimension of transfer pricing. The purpose is to identify, measure, and explain the similarities and differences between the transfer pricing practices of large companies in the United States and Japan. Another goal is to enhance our understanding of the factors entering into the decision-making processes related to transfer pricing in U.S. and Japanese companies.

The book is intended to be useful not only to business executives but also to researchers, teachers, and students in the areas of international business, comparative management, and accounting because it analyzes the more important environmental variables of international transfer pricing and presents the recent experience in transfer pricing of more than 200 large U.S. and Japanese corporations. This information will be very useful for companies trying to establish or revise their transfer pricing policies. This book also presents, for the first time in English, comprehensive statistical evidence of Japanese transfer pricing practices. The exposure to different philosophies and practices provided by this book will help prevent dogmatism and narrowness in building theories for both domestic and international transfer pricing. Therefore, the book can be used as a supplement for courses in comparative management, international accounting, and international financial management.

Because this book is based largely on a doctoral dissertation presented to the University of Nebraska in 1977, I wish to express my gratitude to Professors Robert H. Raymond and C. K. Walter, Cochairmen of the supervisory committee, for their advice, encouragement, and invaluable assistance throughout this research endeavor. They also gave generously of their time to edit the manuscript. Special thanks are also extended to other members of the committee including Professors George C. Holdren, David J. Ellison, John J. Branch, and Steven A. Eggland for their assistance and helpful comments.

This study owes much to many corporate executives from Japan and the United States. Without their cooperation and contribution, the study would not have been completed. Sincere thanks are extended to Mr. Dale A. Hamilton of Peat, Marwick, Mitchell & Co., and Mr. Keith C. Mitchell of Touche Ross and Co. for their contributions.

My appreciation also extends to many other individuals who provided valuable suggestions and assistance to this research. Professors K. H. Chan, Kung H. Chen, Lloyd R. Amey, and Mr. Robert Letvosky deserve special recognition. My thanks are also extended to Mrs. S. L. Marshall, Miss Stella Scalia, and Mrs. Pina Vicario for their help in editing and typing the manuscript.

I also wish to express my deepest appreciation to my wife Ann for the patience and encouragement she provided during the entire period of this study. My daughter Sherri, who shared the stress and strains in completing this research, deserves a special note of appreciation. Finally, this book is dedicated to my parents. The entire experience of higher education would not have been possible without their support, understanding, and continued encouragement.

CONTENTS

LIST OF TABLES

1

INTRODUCTION

THE PROBLEM AND ITS SIGNIFICANCE

The trend toward decentralization and implementation of the profit center or investment center concept has provided increased autonomy at the divisional levels of many business firms.[1] At the same time, it has created the need for a sound transfer pricing system to assist in the optimal allocation of corporate resources. The transfer pricing problems of a domestic company are complicated enough; in a multinational context, the problems take on new and more complex dimensions as a result of variations in tax rates, customs duties, government legislation, business practices, and the like.

Since the mid-1950s, the issues on transfer pricing have been discussed extensively in business literature. Most of the studies, however, deal with the theoretical merits of various pricing methods. More than a dozen empirical studies have been carried out by researchers. A majority of these studies focus on the domestic dimension of the problem, but a few deal with the international aspect of transfer pricing.[2]

Despite the abundance of literature to date, many transfer pricing problems remain unsolved. There is still a shortage of hard empirical evidence on foreign transfer pricing systems, especially Japanese systems. The author's concern regarding the limited empirical data is shared by Itzhak Sharav:

> Admittedly, there has been no systematic long-range monitoring of the transfer pricing policies of multidivisional corporations. The resultant hard empirical data are therefore spotty and in marked contrast to

1

the relative abundance of speculation and theoretical inquiry into the subject.[3]

The last decade witnessed tremendous growth in international trade and the expansion of multinational operations by both U.S. and non-U.S. industrial companies. One source suggests that "about 40 percent of all international trade consists of transfers between related business entities."[4] These signal an urgent need for understanding the problems of adapting domestic transfer pricing systems to conditions abroad, as well as a need for evaluating the assumptions and conditions taken for granted in a domestic context.

The economic role played by the Japanese business community in the international scene has become more and more important during recent years. As shown in Table 1.1, Japan's share of world trade jumped from 5.6 percent in 1967 to 7.4 percent in 1977. Japan is also a major trading partner of the United States. In 1977, the United States imported $19.7 billion worth of goods from Japan whereas U.S. exports to Japan were $12.4 billion, leaving the 1977 U.S. trade deficit with Japan at a record of $7.3 billion.[5]

The huge U.S. trade deficit in 1977 and 1978, plus other factors, has brought about a sharp decline in the value of the U.S. dollar against the Japanese yen, the German mark, and other major European currencies. In addition, the U.S. trade deficit with Japan has created serious trade disputes between the world's two largest capitalist economies, and these disputes have strained overall relations between the two nations.

Because Japanese influences are widely felt in the United States and other countries, their transfer pricing systems, particularly the international dimension of their systems, definitely deserve a closer look. In fact, it is the scarcity of hard empirical data on international transfer pricing and the need for understanding Japanese systems that motivated the author to pursue this study.

DEFINITIONS OF TERMS

Several terms are so important to this study that they ought to be clarified:

Transfer price is the unit price assigned to goods and services transferred between the parent company and subsidiaries or between divisions within the same firm.

Cost-oriented transfer prices are transfer prices derived mainly through cost information as opposed to market price information of products or goods transferred. Examples of cost-oriented transfer prices include actual or variable cost of production, stand-

TABLE 1.1: Japan's Imports and Exports as a Percentage
of World Total for 1967, 1972, and 1977
(money amounts in millions of U.S. dollars)

Exports and Imports	1967	1972	1977
World*	394,800	764,900	2,071,310
Japan	22,105	52,062	152,454
Japan's share of world total	5.6%	6.8%	7.4%

*World trade excludes trade with Eastern Europe, mainland China, North Korea, Vietnam, and Cuba.

Source: International Monetary Fund, International Financial Statistics (Washington, D.C.: IMF, various issues).

ard or actual full-production cost, standard or actual production cost plus a markup.

Market-oriented transfer prices are transfer prices formulated mainly through the market price information of products or services transferred. Examples of market-oriented transfer prices are market price, market price less selling expenses, and the like.

Non-cost-oriented transfer prices include market-oriented transfer prices and other transfer prices not formulated mainly through cost information of products or services transferred. Negotiated transfer price is included in this category.

A multinational company or multinational corporation (MNC) is a company that has at least one subsidiary or branch in one foreign country.

OBJECTIVES AND SCOPE OF THE STUDY

The primary objective of this study is to identify, measure, and explain the similarities and differences in transfer pricing practices of selected industrial companies in the United States and Japan. The following elements of the transfer pricing systems used by companies in these two countries will be compared and contrasted:

Pricing methods: refers to the use of such bases as market price, cost, or negotiated price as transfer prices.

Pricing objectives and the importance the U.S. and Japanese firms place upon major environmental variables when they formulate their international transfer pricing policies.

Other policies and procedures: includes the authority for determining transfer pricing policies, policies on outside purchases of raw materials and intermediate goods, ways of settling disputes among divisions, and so on.

Similarities and differences among the transfer pricing systems of selected firms from the two countries are examined in the light of recent developments in U.S.-Japan bilateral trade, and in the economic and tax environments faced by these companies. Particular attention is paid to possible implications of these similarities and differences for international financial management.

This study also attempts to empirically test the following conclusions stated in Jeffrey S. Arpan's study:[6]

There is a substantial correlation between the firm's size and the transfer pricing system orientation: the larger the parent firm, the more likely it is to use a cost-oriented system.

U.S. systems of international intracorporate pricing are distinctly more cost oriented and more complex than non-U.S. systems.

The very large multinational companies of all nationalities exhibit the smallest differences in system orientation and views of attendant problems. They take into account essentially the same variables and parameters, and they utilize similar techniques.

Some parts of the above conclusions reached by Arpan are restated as hypotheses in this study and are tested using the data obtained from large U.S. and Japanese industrial firms through a questionnaire survey.

Another objective of this study is to discover the extent of application of the decomposition method and other mathematical programming approaches among the large corporations in Japan and the United States. These methods have been explored by many writers since the early 1960s.[7] Large corporations would most likely have the facilities to implement these sophisticated techniques.

RESEARCH HYPOTHESES

Seven hypotheses were tested in this study. For convenience of testing, all hypotheses are stated in null form. The first two

(A-1, A-2) are related to the second Arpan conclusion cited in the previous section.

A-1. The extent of application of cost-oriented or non-cost-oriented <u>domestic</u> transfer prices among large (U.S.) industrial companies (LAIC) and large Japanese industrial companies (LJIC) does not vary according to the nationality of these firms.

A-2. The extent of application of cost-oriented or non-cost-oriented <u>international</u> transfer prices among LAIC and LJIC does not vary according to the nationality of these companies.

The next four hypotheses (B-1, B-2, B-3, B-4) are related to the first Arpan conclusion quoted earlier.

B-1. The extent of usage of cost-oriented transfer prices for <u>domestic</u> interdivisional transfers among LAIC is not related to the size of these companies.

B-2. The extent of usage of cost-oriented transfer prices for <u>domestic</u> interdivisional transfers among LJIC is not related to the size of these companies.

B-3. The extent of usage of cost-oriented transfer prices for <u>international</u> interdivisional transfers among LAIC is not related to the size of these companies.

B-4. The extent of usage of cost-oriented transfer prices for <u>international</u> interdivisional transfers among LJIC is not related to the size of these companies.

The next hypothesis (C-1) is related in part to the third Arpan conclusion cited earlier.

C-1. There is no significant difference between the absolute importance placed upon each of the major environmental variables by LAIC and LJIC when they formulate their international transfer pricing policies.*

RESEARCH METHODS

The research methods used in this study include a thorough review of the literature, a questionnaire survey, and supplemental

---

*In the full-scale questionnaire survey, respondents were asked to rate the importance of 20 environmental variables. Results of the survey are discussed in Chapters 5 and 6.

personal interviews. The purposes of the literature review were to build a solid conceptual foundation for this research and to understand the current economic and tax environments in Japan and the United States. A questionnaire survey was used to gather the empirical data to test the hypotheses and to attain the objectives of this study. To guard against the drawing of unsupported conclusions, the findings and results from the research were discussed with a number of business educators and two experienced partners of international accounting firms. Details of the research design and methodology are described in Chapter 4.

POTENTIAL CONTRIBUTIONS OF THE STUDY

The research will present, for the first time in English literature, some statistical evidence of Japanese transfer pricing practices. Latest information on U.S. transfer pricing systems will also be provided. The potential contribution of this study, however, extends far beyond merely adding to the latest information on international transfer pricing. The cross-national aspect of the study permits analysis of the similarities and differences between the practices of the two national groups and the reasons underlying them. This revelation of some of the ways of solving international transfer pricing problems in the two countries will contribute to a better understanding of management approaches in a variety of environments.

Part of this book analyzes the more important environmental variables of international transfer pricing and presents the recent experience of more than 200 large U.S. and Japanese corporations on transfer pricing. This information will be very useful to those corporations trying to establish their international transfer pricing policies for the first time and for those that are in the process of revising their policies.

The exposure to different philosophies and practices furnished by this book may help prevent dogmatism and narrowness in building theories for both domestic and international transfer pricing. A comparison between the current practices and the theory of transfer pricing should also unveil any potential communication gap that exists between practitioners and researchers. The results of this study may also have some implications for the accounting principle setting bodies in the area of related party transactions.

This research supplies meaningful classroom materials for students in international accounting, managerial accounting, and comparative management. Also, it provides further questions to be investigated by researchers in the future and may point toward better solutions to the complex problems of international transfer pricing.

ORGANIZATION OF THE BOOK

Now that the reader has been given an overview of the problems, objectives, research hypotheses, and potential contribution of the study, it may be helpful to give an advance look at the remainder of the book. As previously mentioned, the second chapter attempts to build a conceptual foundation by reviewing various proposals on proper transfer price(s) and the more recent empirical studies on domestic and international dimensions of transfer pricing.

The third chapter examines major characteristics of the business environment in Japan, which may have a great impact on the transfer pricing practices of Japanese corporations. Recent developments on such important issues as U.S. and Japanese bilateral trade, Japanese trade policies and dumping practices, and the devaluation of the U.S. dollar against the Japanese yen are also discussed.

Research design and methodology are described in Chapter 4. Among other things, this chapter explains how the pilot study and the full-scale study were implemented, and the statistical methods used for inference in the research.

Chapter 5 contains a description of important characteristics of the respondent firms and a thorough analysis of the responses on transfer pricing methods used by the U.S. and Japanese corporations.

Chapter 6 presents the findings of the questionnaire survey on environmental variables and other policies and issues related to transfer pricing. Also included in this chapter are the results from the interviews with two practicing CPAs and the outcome of a nonresponse bias test.

Finally, Chapter 7 presents a summary of the major research findings and conclusions of this study, and suggests further research needed in the areas of domestic and international transfer pricing.

NOTES

1. One survey of the 1976 Fortune "1000" companies shows that 95.8 percent of the respondents used either investment centers or profit centers. See James S. Reece and William R. Cool, "Measuring Investment Center Performance," Harvard Business Review, May-June 1978, pp. 28-30, 34, 36, 40, 42, 46, 174, 176.

2. See, for example, James S. Shulman, "When the Price Is Wrong—By Design," Columbia Journal of World Business 2 (May-June 1967): 69-76; and Jeffrey S. Arpan, International Intracorporate Pricing: Non-American Systems and Views (New York: Praeger, 1972).

3. Itzhak Sharav, "Transfer Pricing—Diversity of Goals and Practices," Journal of Accountancy 137 (April 1974): 56-62.

4. Frederick D. S. Choi and Gerhard G. Mueller, An Introduction to Multinational Accounting (Englewood Cliffs, N.J.: Prentice-Hall, 1978), p. 303.

5. This information was provided by the Consulate General of Japan in New York City.

6. Arpan, op. cit., pp. 79, 109.

7. See, for example, William J. Baumol and Tibor Fabian, "Decomposition, Pricing for Decentralization and External Economics," Management Science 11 (July 1959):429-32; and J. William Petty II and Ernest W. Walker, "Optimal Transfer Pricing for the Multinational Firm," Financial Management 1 (Winter 1972):74-84.

2

REVIEW OF THE LITERATURE

Transfer pricing is a traditionally secretive and yet essential area of corporate management. The pervasiveness of transfer pricing problems can be proven by the existence of a vast and growing literature addressing various aspects of transfer pricing. Thorough discussion of many fundamental issues on transfer pricing can be found in several popular books in managerial accounting.[1] The discussion in this chapter will not attempt to cover all aspects of transfer pricing; rather, it will summarize the important literature in the following areas:

Various proposals on proper transfer price(s)
Empirical studies on domestic transfer pricing
Empirical studies on multinational dimensions of transfer pricing

PROPOSALS ON PROPER TRANSFER PRICE(S)

Selection of the proper transfer price to account for inter-divisional transfers has been a controversial topic in business literature for more than two decades. The diversity of opinions among writers can be seen in Table 2.1. The proposals range from an extreme of doing away with transfer prices under most circumstances to the opposite extreme whereby all methods are acceptable as long as they help accomplish the corporate objectives. The following is a brief review of these proposals.

M. C. Wells dismissed transfer prices and profit centers as mystical inventions that cannot serve as a basis for actions.[2] In another article, Wells reaffirmed his belief that transfer prices serve no useful purpose unless some attempt is to be made to calculate a divisional profit.[3]

TABLE 2.1: A Summary of the Proposals on
Proper Transfer Price(s)

I. Do away with transfer price under most circumstances (Wells
1968, 1971)*
II. Cost-oriented methods:
    A. Economic cost-oriented methods:
        1. Marginal cost: Hirshleifer (1956)
        2. Opportunity cost: Samuels (1965); Onsi (1970);
           Holstrum and Sauls (1973)
    B. Accounting cost or cost-plus methods:
        1. Incremental cost: Goetz (1967)
        2. Cost plus some allowance for profit: Gordon (1970);
           Vendig (1973)
III. Market-oriented methods:
    Market price: Cook (1955); also proposed by Hirshleifer
    (1956) under some circumstances
IV. Negotiated price: Dean (1955); Li (1965); Haidinger (1970);
Fremgen (1970); Shaub (1978)
V. Dual pricing: Drebin (1959); Greer (1962); Edwards and
Roemmich (1976)
VI. Mathematical programming:
    A. The decomposition procedure: Dantzig and Wolfe (1960);
        Baumol and Fabian (1964); Hass (1964)
    B. Linear programming approach: Petty and Walker (1972)
    C. Other method: Rutenberg (1970)
VII. Different prices for different purposes: Bierman (1959)

---

*The years in the parentheses show the years the writers'
articles or books were published. Details of the references can be
found in various footnotes of this chapter and in the Bibliography.
    Source: Compiled by the author.

    Wells did not give recognition to the fact that calculation of
divisional profits is but one of the many purposes served by a transfer
pricing system. Transfer pricing information can be used for making
a number of decisions, including make-or-buy, capital budgeting,
and pricing decisions of finished products.
    In one article, Jack Hirshleifer proposed the following rules
for determining transfer prices:[4]

    If the intermediate market is competitive, the transfer price
should be the market price.

If the market for the intermediate commodity is imperfectly competitive, the transfer price should be the marginal manufacturing cost of the manufacturing division.

Several other writers have proposed another economic cost method, that is, the opportunity cost approach.[5] By this approach, if there is an outside market price, the goods transferred are priced at the market price, which represents the opportunity cost of not selling to outsiders. If there is no market price, the transferred goods should be priced at the opportunity cost of diverting the resources of the production division into manufacturing a particular product rather than producing another kind of good that has an outside market.

Both the marginal cost and the opportunity cost proposals are conceptually sound and all have theoretical merits. However, it is difficult to use the two approaches in real world situations because accurate demand functions and cost functions are not easy to estimate. The exact opportunity cost of a particular resource can hardly be determined. This is more evident in the case of international transfer pricing than in domestic transfer pricing.

Billy E. Goetz recommended the use of incremental cost, which is the cost that changes as a result of a proposed action or decision.[6] Two cost-plus methods were proposed by Myron J. Gordon and R. E. Vendig.[7] Gordon's proposal was recommended for the decentralized administration of a socialist economy. Vendig called his proposal a "three-part transfer price" because the price included three distinct categories: standard variable manufacturing cost, a lump-sum payment representing a portion of traceable budgeted fixed costs, and a charge for the use of capital employed.

Goetz's incremental cost proposal could be relevant to internal decision making. However, it may violate the regulations under Section 482 of the Internal Revenue Code. According to this regulation, only the following four groups of methods may be used to determine the transfer price:[8]

The comparable uncontrolled price method
The resale method
The cost-plus method
Some appropriate method when none of the methods described above can reasonably be applied under the facts and circumstances as they exist in a particular case

Vendig's method is acceptable for tax purposes.

Many writers, including Hirshleifer[9] and P. W. Cook,[10] advocated the use of actual market price as the transfer price if a competitive market for intermediate products exists. The market-oriented approach is an attempt to approximate an arm's length, bargained, open-market price. There are problems, however, in using market price as a basis for transfer prices. Many intermediate products do not have competitive markets. Strictly comparable market prices are rare because of differences in quality, credit terms, terms of delivery, and services.

The use of negotiated prices was recommended by Joel Dean, David H. Li, Timothy P. Haidinger, James M. Fremgen, and H. James Shaub.[11] Dean maintained that transfer pricing must preserve the profit-making autonomy of the division manager so that his selfish interests will be identical with the interests of the company as a whole. Prices negotiated in arm's length bargaining by divisional managers will help accomplish this goal. Similar arguments for negotiated prices were presented by Li, Haidinger, Fregmen, and Shaub in their respective articles.

Negotiated transfer price is compatible with profit decentralization. It restores the divisional managers' freedom of action and thereby increases their accountability for profits. But one of the drawbacks of negotiated price is that it may involve time-consuming negotiation.

Dual pricing is the use of two transfer prices. One price will be used to charge the buying (or receiving) division for the transfers whereas the selling (or producing) division will be credited with another. Three variations of dual pricing were proposed by Allen R. Drebin, Howard C. Greer, James Don Edwards, and Roger A. Roemmich.[12] For example, Drebin proposed that the buying division be charged with marginal cost whereas the selling division should be credited for selling price minus profits and cost of completion.[13]

One of the key arguments for using dual pricing is that two sets of transfer prices would accomplish more objectives than would a single transfer price. Nevertheless, some authors caution against the use of dual pricing. Charles H. Horngren warned that "the looseness of dual pricing may gradually induce unwelcome attitudes and practices."[14]

Some writers have discussed the applications of mathematical programming in transfer pricing, and various models have been proposed. The decomposition procedure developed by W. J. Baumol and T. Fabian takes advantage of the economies of decentralized decision making by divisions within a large company.[15] J. William Petty and Ernest W. Walker built a linear programming model to determine the optimal transfer price for a multinational firm.[16] David P. Rutenberg's model deals with the optimal use of tax havens, bilateral tax treaties, nonuniform treatments of income received from abroad, and national differences in income tax rates, import duties, and border taxes.[17] These writers identified the key determinants of transfer pricing, and their arguments for using mathematical programming seem plausible. However, their assumptions are often very restrictive. For example, the assumption of linearity of linear programming limits the application of the model to many real world problems. These are probably the major reasons that mathematical programming methods are not widely used in practice to determine transfer prices.

Harold Bierman, Jr. took the stand that no one transfer price can satisfy the needs of a decentralized corporation and the selection of transfer prices for a firm is dependent largely upon the uses of transfer pricing information.[18] Bierman considered market price the best for measuring performance whereas marginal cost (variable cost) or differential cost is best for making such decisions as "make or buy," pricing, capital budgeting, and so on. Full cost must be used for general financial accounting according to the generally accepted accounting principles.

If a firm finds it desirable to use its transfer pricing information for more than one objective, it follows that the firm has to use either dual pricing or more than two transfer prices. This may explain why many industrial firms are using more than one transfer price today.

EMPIRICAL STUDIES ON DOMESTIC
TRANSFER PRICING

Table 2.2 summarizes the major empirical studies related to transfer pricing practices within one single country. These studies have been carried out since the middle part of the 1950s. Because of limited space, only studies done in the 1960s and 1970s will be reviewed according to the chronological sequence of their publications or year of dissertation.

Solomons's Study

The purpose of the study by David Solomons was to investigate the financial relations existing between the central management of a divisionalized company and the management of its several divisions.[19]

Chapter 6 of Solomons's report discusses interdivisional relationships, which tie closely to transfer pricing. The most common methods used among his sample firms were market price or market price less selling expenses. Marginal cost was used by only one company as a supplementary method.[20]

TABLE 2.2: Summary of the Major Empirical Studies on Domestic Transfer Pricing

Author (or Sponsor) and Year of Publication*	Key Method(s) Used	Respondents
National Association of Accountants (1956)	Interviews	40 U.S. companies characterized by integrated operations and multiunit organization
Stone (1957)	Questionnaire survey and interviews	332 large U.S. manufacturing companies
Solomons (1965)	Interviews	25 U.S. industrial companies
National Conference Board (1967)	Questionnaire survey	190 U.S. corporations
Mautz (1968)	Questionnaire survey	412 companies and 218 financial analysts
Piper (1969)	Questionnaire survey	55 British companies
Larson (1974)	Interviews	8 U.S. companies
Olpechi (1976)	Questionnaire	67 manufacturing companies in Ohio
Emmanuel (1977)	Questionnaire	Just over 100 British companies

*References can be found in various notes of this chapter and in the Bibliography.

Source: Compiled by the author.

Solomons stressed two aspects of transfer pricing in his discussion: performance evaluation and goal congruence. He stated:

> Since transfer prices are an essential part of the profit measurement system, they must, as accurately as possible, help management to evaluate the performance of the profit centers viewed as separate entities. They must also motivate them to act in a manner which is conducive to the success of the company as a whole. [21]

In his report, Solomons also discussed the decision rules for using various prices under a number of conditions.

The 1967 Conference Board Study

The 1967 Conference Board study was based upon the experience of 190 companies and was limited to transfers of goods among domestic divisions of industrial corporations. [22] The study indicated that the use of more than one transfer pricing method was common among the firms surveyed. Two-thirds of the firms used some form of cost method, either as the sole pricing basis or in combination with market-based prices. At the same time, more than half of the firms surveyed used market-based transfer price either alone or in combination with some form of cost method.

Most companies in the study allowed outside purchases of raw materials and intermediate goods after obtaining specific permission from corporate management. Inadequacy of internal production and more favorable outside prices are the most common reasons for permitting outside purchases.

Mautz's Study

Part of Robert K. Mautz's study was related to transfer pricing. [23] Of the 404 companies responding to the questions on intracompany pricing in Mautz's survey, 341 companies (84 percent) used at least one method of transfer pricing. A variety of transfer prices was used by the companies that used transfer prices, and no single method seemed to dominate the others. Of the 341 companies that had transfer prices, 166 companies (49 percent) used only one method, 80 firms (23 percent) used two transfer prices; others used more than two prices.

Piper's Study

Fifty-five British companies responded to A. G. Piper's survey.[24] Twenty-nine corporations (53 percent) used market-oriented transfer prices. These prices were either market price or market price adjusted for freight, quantity discount, or other factors. A large number of firms allowed their divisions to negotiate a transfer price. But the negotiation was usually concerned with establishing a market price, and adjustments thereto were made to reflect savings from trading internally. Piper found no evidence to suggest that the mathematical programming techniques were used by even the largest British companies.

Larson's Study

Raymond L. Larson conducted in-depth interviews with eight companies.[25] All of the companies advocated market price as the best method of pricing intracompany transfers; however, none of them used it. Except for a few situations in which established markets did exist, transfer prices were largely arbitrary among the companies Larson interviewed.

Policies on outside purchases of intermediate or final products were found to be very restrictive. It was only when the producing division lacked the capacity to meet the demand that units were allowed to purchase in local markets after obtaining approval from top management.

Okpechi's Study

The purpose of S. O. Okpechi's study was to examine the conflict of the interest dilemma among divisional managers in a transfer pricing context.[26] Empirical facts were gathered mainly through a questionnaire survey.

Full actual cost was found to be the most widely used transfer price; it was used by 32 percent of the respondents. Standard cost was used by 19 percent of the respondents, negotiated market price by 17 percent, and full cost-plus by 15 percent of the respondents. None of them used either marginal cost or shadow prices.

Okpechi found that the four major sources of conflict in a transfer pricing situation were allocation of corporate resources, coordination of the flow of materials between divisions, differences among divisional goals, and overemphasis on individual manager performance.[27]

Emmanuel's Study

About 100 large British companies participated in Clive Emmanuel's survey.[28] Emmanuel found that "40 percent of the companies expressed dissatisfaction with their present form of transfer price and of the remaining 60 percent, 25 percent expressed satisfaction with the market-oriented transfer prices because the amounts traded internally are relatively small."[29] Emmanuel found that there was no significant relationship between the individual form of transfer price used and the response of satisfaction or dissatisfaction. Each of the market-oriented transfer prices was perceived as having some limitations.

EMPIRICAL STUDIES ON THE MULTINATIONAL DIMENSIONS OF TRANSFER PRICING

The last two decades have witnessed tremendous growth in MNCs and international trade. Many large corporations established overseas subsidiaries to take advantage of the opportunities in foreign markets. This created some complex problems for international transfer pricing. Table 2.3 summarizes the major empirical studies related to the multinational dimensions of transfer pricing. Again, these studies will be discussed according to the chronological sequence of their publications or year of dissertation.

The 1965 Business International Corporation
(BIC) Study

The purpose of the 1956 Business International Corporation (BIC) study was to examine various aspects of pricing problems faced by international businesses.[30] Chapter 3 of that report deals specifically with international transfer pricing.

After analyzing the practices of more than 30 U.S. MNCs, BIC found "a distinct popularity for transfer prices based either on local plant production cost plus a fixed percentage mark-up, or on plant production cost of the most efficient manufacturing unit in the corporate group plus a fixed percentage mark-up, regardless of individual plant costs."[31] A number of variables that affect international transfer prices were discussed in the report. These variables include antidumping legislation, interests of local joint venture partners, tax and customs duties considerations.

TABLE 2.3: Summary of the Major Empirical Studies on Multinational Dimensions of Transfer Pricing

Author (or Sponsor) and Year of Publication*	Key Method(s) Used	Respondents
The 1965 BIC study	Interview	International corporations (number not available)
Shulman's study (1966)	Interview	8 large U.S. manufacturing companies having large amount of investment overseas
Bisat's study (1966)	Questionnaire	14 CPAs from the large accounting firms in the United States, Canada, and the Netherlands
Greene and Duerrs' study (1970)	Questionnaire survey	Executives from 130 companies
Arpan's study (1972)	Questionnaire survey	60 wholly owned U.S. subsidiaries of foreign firms
The 1973 BIC study	Interview	International corporations (number not available)
Milburn's study (1977)	Questionnaire survey and interview	33 partners from the major accounting firms in Canada and the United States

*References can be found in various footnotes in this chapter and in the Bibliography.

Source: Compiled by the author.

Shulman's Study

In his study, James S. Shulman examined the transfer pricing mechanism of multinational business and identified the opportunities and dangers in the international environment.[32] He discussed the major environmental variables affecting international transfer pricing. These include income taxes, import duties, currency fluctuation, economic restrictions imposed by host countries, competitive positions of foreign subsidiaries, and so forth. All the firms interviewed acknowledged the existence of these variables but not all of them elected to consider these variables in transfer pricing.

Shulman emphasized the need for maintaining a functional control system to measure, evaluate, and motivate divisional management. He concluded that a successful transfer pricing method in multinational business should not cause destructive changes in the existing control system.

Bisat's Study

The main purpose of Talal A. Bisat's study was to estimate the extent of intercompany transactions in international trade and to evaluate the function of the public accountant regarding the effects of such transactions and pricing on the financial statements of MNCs.[33]

Bisat analyzed the expansion of international business between 1946 and 1965, and found that the problem of transfer pricing had been very significant in the international economy, of which a substantial and a rising share was represented by intercompany transactions. Such transactions were conservatively estimated to account for close to one-third of the non-Communist world's foreign trade in merchandise.

Another significant finding was that independent auditors exercise little influence on the valuation of intercompany transactions. No professional responsibility was specifically recognized in this regard by the accounting profession and no guide existed for the performance of such a function.

Greene and Duerrs' Study

The study by James Greene and Michael G. Duerr focused on the international transfer pricing practices of 130 MNCs.[34] The results showed that tax and customs considerations and the desires of domestic divisional executives and local managers abroad have a profound influence on corporate policy in international transfer pricing.

Nearly all the respondents reported that their transfer pricing policies were under constant internal and external pressures, and "counterbalancing these internal and external pressures in ways that will permit the company to operate routinely and grow profitably against competition from other producers" was the major corporate goal of these policies.[35]

The survey indicated that transfer prices were usually established either on a cost-plus basis or by negotiation between the parties involved, depending upon whether the goods could be purchased from outside sources. If the goods could be purchased from outside sources, a negotiated transfer price was used. Otherwise, a cost-plus transfer price was normally used.

Arpan's Study

The study by Arpan was one of the few studies on non-U.S. transfer pricing systems.[36] The subjects of his questionnaire survey were the wholly owned U.S. subsidiaries of foreign firms. Sixty companies representing ten countries responded to his survey. Some key findings and conclusions of his research were described in Chapter 1 and were restated as hypotheses to be tested in this study.

In Arpan's study, 30 respondents classified their systems' orientation. "Seventeen firms reported an arm's-length (market price) method, three claimed a market-price-less commission system, four mentioned a cost-plus arrangement, and six called theirs a combination system."[37]

As to the differences in national preferences, Arpan made the following conclusions:

The French prefer non-market-oriented systems because they can thus minimize world tax payments. The English also prefer a cost orientation, but their goal is to achieve their target return on investment rates. The Italians use market-oriented systems to maximize corporate income in Italy, which is equivalent to minimizing their tax liability. Canadians also employ market-oriented systems, but essentially because of specific government regulations and a desire to maintain good relations with other governments. The Scandinavian firms view good relations with other governments as paramount, and consequently they are the biggest supporters and users of market-oriented systems. The Germans are the least concerned about transfer pricing, do not seem to prefer any given orientation, and do not exhibit any dominant pattern.[38]

The 1973 BIC Study

The 1973 BIC study may be regarded as an extension of the 1965 BIC study.[39] The report included an interesting discussion of the problems involved in interdivisional transfers of intangible items such as patents, trademarks, technology, and services.

BIC recognized that pricing of intangibles is one of the most politically sensitive questions faced by MNCs. It offered three key points for establishing transfer prices on intangibles:[40]

Transfer prices for intangibles are based on market value or they are essentially arbitrary.

From a strict licensing point of view, an independent and an affiliated licensee are in an identical position in regard to profitable exploitation of intangible property.

The key external restraint on pricing intangibles is taxes.

Milburn's Study

The study by J. Alex Milburn was concerned with the measurement of transfer transactions between controlled affiliates (national segments) of MNCs.[41] Particular emphasis was devoted to the external user of national segment financial data in Canada and the United States.

Milburn found that intracompany transfers between the Canadian companies and their foreign parents or other affiliates accounted for significant portions of both the U.S. and Canadian exports and imports, and that the reported operating results of major Canadian companies were highly sensitive to international transfer pricing variability.

In one article, Milburn suggested that the Canadian accounting profession should concentrate on developing disclosures to help financial statement users make informed decisions as to the impact of international transfer transactions on company results.[42]

SUMMARY AND EVALUATION

More than 100 articles have been written and more than a dozen empirical studies carried out in the past on transfer pricing, but essential empirical data are still lacking. A review of the various proposals on transfer price leads to the conclusion that a single transfer price can hardly meet all the objectives of a large corporation. More than one transfer price is needed to accomplish the objectives of maximizing corporate profit, measuring divisional performance, determining income of each division and that of the whole company, and minimizing worldwide tax payments. The popularity of multiple transfer prices among companies participating in past empirical studies supported this contention.

In this chapter, 16 empirical studies were identified. Of them, nine dealt with the practices in one single country. Others involved the multinational dimension of transfer pricing. All of these studies provided some insight into the various aspects of transfer pricing. The two BIC studies, Shulman's research, the study by Greene and Duerr, and Arpan's study are particularly helpful in identifying and analyzing the key environmental variables influencing international transfer pricing practices. Arpan's study also provides some insight into the non-U.S. systems. The studies by Bisat and Milburn deal with the financial accounting aspect of transfer pricing and their recommendations are worthy of consideration.

There are, however, a number of limitations to the above studies. The samples used by Shulman and Bisat were too small for their conclusions to be generalized. Eight companies participated in Shulman's study, and 14 public accountants and several accounting professors took part in Bisat's study. Arpan collected his information from the U.S. subsidiaries of foreign firms. The views of these subsidiaries were unlikely to be exactly the same as those of their parent companies. One of the major limitations of Arpan's study is the lack of responses from Japanese firms in his survey.

The spectacular growth of the Japanese economy and foreign trade since the early 1950s has brought admiration and complaints against the Japanese business community. Since Japan has been one of our major trading partners and one of our political allies since the end of World War II, Japanese transfer pricing practices deserve more attention than has been given them in the past. One of the major objectives is to provide readers with recent information on Japanese practices.

NOTES

1. See, for example, Charles T. Horngren, Cost Accounting: A Managerial Emphasis (Englewood Cliffs, N.J.: Prentice-Hall, 1977), pp. 673-92; Gordon Shillinglaw, Managerial Cost Accounting (Homewood, Ill.: Irwin, 1977), pp. 847-71; and David Solomons, Divisional Performance: Measurement and Control (Homewood, Ill.: Irwin, 1965), pp. 160-211.

2. M. C. Wells, "Profit Centers, Transfer Prices and Mysticism," Abacus 4 (December 1968): 180.

3. M. C. Wells, "Transfer Prices and Profit Center? No," Abacus 7 (June 1971): 56.

4. Jack Hirshleifer, "On the Economics of Transfer Pricing," Journal of Business 29 (July 1956): 176, 179.

5. See, for example, Mohamed Onsi, "A Transfer Pricing System Based on Opportunity Cost," Accounting Review 45 (July 1970): 535-43; and Gary L. Holstrum and E. H. Sauls, "The Opportunity Cost Transfer Price," Management Accounting 54 (May 1973): 29-33.

6. Billy E. Goetz, "Transfer Prices: An Exercise in Relevancy and Goal Congruence," Accounting Review 42 (July 1967): 435-70.

7. Myron J. Gordon, "A Method of Pricing for a Socialist Economy," Accounting Review 45 (July 1970): 427-43; R. E. Vendig, "A Three-Part Transfer Price," Management Accounting 55 (September 1973): 33-36.

8. "Allocation of Income and Deductions Among Taxpayers: Determination of Source of Income (Section 482, IRC)," Federal Register, April 16, 1968.

9. Hirshleifer, op. cit.

10. Paul W. Cook, "Decentralization and Transfer-Price Problem," Journal of Business 28 (April 1955): 87-94.

11. Joel Dean, "Decentralization and Intracompany Pricing," Harvard Business Review 33 (July-August 1955): 65-74; David H. Li, "Interdivisional Transfer Planning," Management Accounting 46 (June 1965): 51-54; Timothy P. Haidinger, "Negotiate for Profits," Management Accounting 52 (December 1970): 23-24, 52; James M. Fremgen, "Transfer Pricing and Management Goal," Management Accounting 52 (December 1970): 25-31; and H. James Shaub, "Transfer Pricing in a Decentralized Organization," Management Accounting 59 (April 1978): 33-36, 42.

12. Allen R. Drebin, "A Proposal for Dual Pricing of Intracompany Transfers," NAA Bulletin 40 (February 1959): 51-55; Howard C. Greer, "Divisional Profit Calculation, Notes on the 'Transfer Rate' Problem," NAA Bulletin 43 (July 1962): 5-12; and James Don Edwards and Roger A. Roemmich, "Transfer Pricing: The Wrong Tool for Performance Evaluation," Cost and Management 50 (January-February 1976): 35-37.

13. Drebin, op. cit., p. 54.

14. Horngren, op. cit., p. 689.

15. William J. Baumol and Tibor Fabian, "Decomposition, Pricing for Decentralization and External Economics," Management Science 11 (September 1964): 1-32.

16. J. William Petty, II and Ernest W. Walker, "Optimal Transfer Pricing for the Multinational Firm," Financial Management 1 (Winter 1972): 74-84.

17. David P. Rutenberg, "Maneuvering Liquid Assets in a Multinational Company: Formulation and Deterministic Solution Procedures," Management Science 16 (June 1970): B671-B684.

18. Harold Bierman Jr., "Pricing Intracompany Transfer," Accounting Review 34 (July 1959): 429-32.

19. Solomons, op. cit.

20. Ibid., p. 183.

21. Ibid., p. 166.

22. National Industrial Conference Board, Interdivisional Transfer Pricing (New York: The Conference Board, 1967).

23. Robert K. Mautz, Financial Reporting by Diversified Companies (New York: Financial Executives Research Foundation, 1968), pp. 33-40.

24. A. G. Piper, "Internal Trading," Accountancy 80 (October 1969): 733-36.

25. Raymond L. Larson, "Decentralization in Real Life," Management Accounting 55 (March 1974): 28-32.

26. Simeon O. Okpechi, "Interdivisional Transfer-Pricing: A Conflict Resolution Approach" (Ph.D. dissertation, The Ohio State University, 1976).

27. Ibid., p. 94.

28. Clive Emmanuel, "Transfer Pricing: A Diagnosis and Possible Solution to Dysfunctional Decision-Making in the Divisionalized Company," Management International Review 17 (1977/4): 45-59.

29. Ibid.

30. Business International Corporation. Solving International Pricing Problems (New York, 1965).

31. Ibid., p. 19.

32. James S. Shulman, "Transfer Pricing in Multinational Business" (Ph.D. dissertation, Harvard University, 1966); also see James S. Shulman, "When the Price is Wrong—By Design," Columbia Journal of World Business 2 (May-June 1967): 69-76.

33. Talal A. Bisat, "An Evaluation of International Intercompany Transactions" (Ph.D. dissertation, American University, 1967).

34. James Greene and Michael G. Duerr, Intercompany Transactions in the Multinational Firm (New York: The Conference Board, 1970).

35. Ibid., pp. vi-vii.

36. Jeffrey S. Arpan, International Intracorporate Pricing: Non-American Systems and Views (New York: Praeger, 1972).

37. Ibid., p. 78.

38. Ibid., p. 105.

39. Business International Corporation, Setting Intercorporate Pricing Policies (New York: BIC, 1973).

40. Ibid., p. 58.

41. J. Alex Milburn, "International Transfer Pricing in a Financial Accounting Context" (Ph.D. dissertation, University of Illinois at Urbana-Champaign, 1977).

42. J. Alex Milburn, "International Transfer Transactions: What Price?" CA Magazine 109 (December 1976): 26.

3

JAPANESE BUSINESS ENVIRONMENT AND U.S.-JAPANESE BILATERAL ECONOMIC ISSUES

A key to understanding both Japanese transfer pricing practices and the differences between U.S. and Japanese transfer pricing systems is to have some knowledge of the Japanese business environment and of the vital bilateral economic issues confronting the two nations. The purpose of this chapter is to provide essential background information in these areas.

The discussion in this chapter will be divided into two parts. The first part covers the following aspects of the Japanese business environment:

Corporate income taxes and withholding taxes
Tariff systems and import restrictions
Antitrust legislation
Existing evidence of Japanese transfer pricing practices
Some accounting rules influencing Japanese transfer pricing practices

Many of these may have significant impact upon the transfer pricing practices of large corporations. In the second part of the chapter, some bilateral economic issues facing the two countries will be examined. These issues include bilateral trade, dumping practices of Japanese firms, U.S. antidumping investigations, and devaluation of the U.S. dollar against the Japanese yen.

SOME ASPECTS OF THE JAPANESE BUSINESS ENVIRONMENT

Corporate Income Taxes and Withholding Taxes

The Japanese corporate income tax system is as complex as its counterpart in the United States. Corporate income taxes in Japan are made up of corporation tax, enterprise tax, prefectural inhabitant tax, and municipal inhabitant tax. [1]

A corporation tax is imposed on the taxable income of corporations. The rates of the corporation tax are 40 percent (or 28 percent) on undistributed profits and 30 percent (or 22 percent) on profits distributed as dividends. The lower rates apply to corporations with an income of no more than ¥7 million and capital of no more than ¥100 million.

The enterprise tax is levied on Japanese-source income, usually at the rate of 6 percent on the first ¥3.5 million, 9 percent on the next ¥3.5 million, and 12 percent on taxable income over ¥7 million. Enterprise tax actually paid can be deducted in computing taxable income for both the corporation tax and enterprise tax itself in the following business year.

Inhabitant taxes are levied by the prefectures and municipalities, which may select an inhabitant tax rate within the following range:

Prefecture	5.2 to 6.2 percent
Municipality	12.1 to 14.5 percent
Tokyo metropolitan (combined)	17.3 to 20.7 percent

These inhabitant taxes are not deductible in computing the corporation tax.

As a nation involved heavily in international trade, Japan encourages exports through many tax incentives. For instance, exporting firms are allowed special reserves for developing overseas markets. Also, these firms are allowed certain special deductions from revenues received in foreign exchange or its equivalent from foreign transactions. [2]

The withholding tax rates on corporate payments of dividends, interest, and royalties are shown in Table 3.1. Since the United States has concluded tax treaties with Japan, special concessions have been granted under these treaties to U.S. corporations. By August 1977, Japan had entered into tax treaties with 28 countries to avoid double taxation. [3]

Tariff System and Import Restrictions

The first Japanese postwar tariff legislation was put into effect in 1951. Since then, several extensive revisions have been made.

TABLE 3.1: Withholding Tax Rates of Japan on Payments
of Dividends, Interest, and Royalties
(percent)

Recipient	Dividends (portfolio)	Dividends (substantial holdings)	Interest	Royalties
Japanese corporations	15	15	15	0
Corporations of foreign countries without tax treaties	20	20	20	20
U.S. corporations	15	10*	10	10

*There are several requirements for the application of this
10 percent tax rate. One requirement is that the U.S. corporation
that receives the dividends must own at least 10 percent of the voting
shares of the Japanese corporation. Consult the United States–Japan
tax treaty for other requirements.

Note: These tax rates were in effect as of August 1, 1977.

Source: Compiled by the author.

Throughout the 1950s, Japan maintained strict control of imported
goods. For the most part, control during this period was implemented through quantitative restrictions.

During the 1960s, Japan gradually removed many of its import
restrictions. Tariff rates were reduced substantially for many
products during the second half of the 1960s. Japan participated in
the Kennedy round of multilateral trade negotiations in the middle
part of that decade. By the end of the negotiations, Japan's average
rates of tariffs were comparable with those of other industrialized
nations.[4]

There are four kinds of tariff rates in the Japanese system:
basic rate, conventional rate, preferential rate, and provisional
rate. The basic rate is stipulated in the Customs Tariff Law and
remains in effect over a long period. The conventional rate is applied
to imports from countries with which Japan maintains a General
Agreement on Tariffs and Trade (GATT) relationship and from coun-

tries with which Japan has agreements that include the most-favored nation treatment in relation to tariffs. The conventional rate is lower than the basic rate.

The preferential rate is the rate applied to imports from developing countries based on agreements worked out at the United Nations Conference on Trade and Development. The provisional rate is a rate temporarily put into effect in place of the basic rate to cope with abnormal situations in the economy. In general, a provisional rate is allowed to be in effect for up to one year. The order of precedence in applying the above four tariff rates is preference rate, conventional rate, provisional rate, and basic rate.

As of January 1978, Japan still had import restrictions on 27 categories of items, most of which are agricultural products. Since then, Japan has taken major steps to cut tariffs and to ease restrictions on imports. In March 1978, as part of an agreement reached with the United States, Japan cut tariffs unilaterally on 124 items with a total estimated import value of $2.1 billion. These 124 items include automobiles, computers, color films, and instant coffee.[5] In addition, Japan removed quotas on 12 products, of which 11 are agricultural. Efforts have also been made to simplify the inspection procedures for imported goods and to remove other nontariff barriers.

Antitrust Legislation

The first Japanese Antimonopoly and Fair Trade Law was passed in 1947. This law, modeled after U.S. antitrust legislation and Supreme Court decisions, prohibited three kinds of practices: private monopolization, unreasonable trade restraints, and unfair business practices. However, the law was rarely enforced during the earlier postwar years because it was too complicated and too foreign to the traditional Japanese economic environment. Some industries have received legislative exemption from the Antimonopoly Law. During the first 16 years of the act, only five allegations of private monopolization were made by the Federal Trade Commission (FTC) of Japan.[6] A revised Antimonopoly law was passed by the Upper House of Japanese Parliament in May 1977. It gives Japan's FTC new power that enables it, for the first time, to break up companies it considers monopolistic. Companies affected are those with total domestic sales exceeding ¥50 billion and having 50 percent or more of the market share in their respective industries (or, together with another firm, more than 75 percent of the market).

By the time the law was passed, the FTC, in anticipation of its new power, had already specified nine industries in which it considered monopolies existed. These included beer, photographic film, sheet glass, tin plate, and wristwatches.[7]

In the early part of 1977, the Japanese and U.S. governments were in the process of negotiating an antitrust agreement as a result of a proposal made by the U.S. Justice Department calling for the two countries to cooperate more closely in supervising and controlling their respective international companies. The more important issues involved are mergers, cartels, licensing agreements, exclusive distributorship, and so forth. A similar agreement between the United States and the German Federal Republic was signed in June 1976.

Existing Evidence of Japanese Transfer
Pricing Practices

There is only a handful of evidence on Japanese transfer pricing practices in English literature. Based primarily on his interviews with eight partners in the "Big Eight" accounting firms, Arpan made the following observation on the Japanese transfer pricing system:

> The Japanese prefer cost-oriented systems, primarily
> from price-competitive reasons. No statistical support
> can be given for this preference because none of the
> Japanese firms participated in this [Arpan's] study.
> The international accountants were aware of this pattern,
> however, and the "dumping" suits brought by the United
> States against the Japanese would seem to bear it out. [8]

Other important findings in Arpan's study have been described in Chapters 1 and 2.

In a study on the pattern of organizational evolution of 50 major Japanese manufacturing companies, M. Y. Yoshino found that transfer price was a frequent source of conflict between Japanese parent companies and their joint venture partners in foreign subsidiaries, especially during the early stages of these joint ventures. [9] During these stages, the joint ventures are heavily dependent on the Japanese parent companies for supplies of materials and components. The foreign partners are anxious to obtain the lowest possible transfer prices for these items to assure that maximum profit is accrued to the joint venture.

Some Accounting Rules Influencing Japanese
Transfer Pricing Practices

Some accounting principles in Japan are different from those used in the United States because of the unique features in each country's economic environment. One of these differences had significant implications for transfer pricing.

Before April 1, 1977, the preparation of consolidated financial statements for a parent company and its subsidiaries was not mandatory in Japan. In the United States, consolidated statements were mandatory as early as 1959.[10] Because of the lack of requirements for consolidated statements, and because the Japanese Commercial Code did not prohibit accrual of intercompany sales and profits, some companies used the opportunity to smooth their earnings or to make the parent-only statements look good by selling products to subsidiaries at inflated prices.

After about 10 years of deliberation, the Business Accounting Principles Board* issued its final opinion on consolidated financial statements on June 24, 1975. According to the Opinion, "Any company having to report under the Securities Exchange Law must consolidate its accounts with those of the company or companies in which it holds more than 50 percent of the issued stock, directly or indirectly, effective for fiscal periods ending after April 1, 1977."[11] The Opinion also stated that the consolidated statements are to be submitted as a supplement to the parent-only statements and audited by certified public accountants. The rules for preparing consolidated financial statements established by the Ministry of Finance also specify that the equity method must be applied in accounting for investment in 20-percent- to 50-percent-owned affiliates and unconsolidated subsidiaries.[12]

About 600 of the largest companies in Japan will be affected by the Opinion of the Business Accounting Principles Board and the rules of the Ministry of Finance. One research center estimated that 60 percent or more of the largest Japanese companies will show drastically reduced profits under the new rule.[13]

U.S.-JAPANESE BILATERAL
ECONOMIC ISSUES

Bilateral Trade

The United States has been the most important trading partner of Japan since the early 1977s. During 1977, Japanese exports to the United States accounted for 24 percent of Japan's total exports,

---

*A majority of the members of the Business Accounting Principles Board are scholars in accounting.

whereas the share of the United States in Japan's total imports was 17 percent. Japan's shares of the U.S. exports and imports for the same year were 10 percent and 13 percent, respectively. Evidently, trade between the two countries is more important to Japan than to the United States.

Japan's exports to the United States increased significantly in 1977. As shown in Table 3.2, Japan's exports to the United States in 1977 achieved an increase of 25.7 percent over the preceding year, to $19.7 billion. In contrast, imports from the United States only increased by 5 percent, to $12.4 billion. Consequently, the U.S. trade deficit with Japan in 1977 was $7.3 billion compared to a deficit of $3.9 billion in 1976.

An examination of Japan's exports to the United States by commodity shows that in 1977 machinery and equipment and metal products accounted for 84.5 percent of the total. The value of shipments of machinery and equipment, including automobiles, to the United States in 1977 increased by 30.8 percent over 1976.

Three commodity categories accounted for 70.2 percent of U.S. exports to Japan in 1977. These categories are raw materials, foodstuffs, and machinery and equipment. Only U.S. exports of raw materials posted a significant gain in 1977, rising 14.3 percent over the preceding year.

The U.S. trade deficit with Japan is expected to worsen in 1978. One source estimated that it may exceed $12 billion.[14] In response to mounting pressure from the U.S. and the European Economic Community (EEC) to reduce the sizable Japanese trade surplus, Japan has taken a number of measures, which include the following:

Maintaining a 7 percent economic growth rate in fiscal year 1979 to expand domestic demand for foreign goods

Reducing tariffs unilaterally on 124 items of goods

Buying an unspecified number of airplanes, nuclear generators, and other industrial products from the United States

Doubling its foreign aid to developing countries within three years

Stockpiling petroleum and other natural resources, buying U.S. uranium, and paying in advance for services to be delivered later

Restricting exports of such major goods as automobiles, steel, and color television receivers to the same level as or below the volume of the fiscal year ended on March 31, 1978

Establishing jointly with the U.S. government, a U.S.-Japanese Trade Facilitation Committee to resolve specific market access

TABLE 3.2: Japanese Exports and Imports
from the United States, 1976–77
(money amount in millions of U.S. dollars)

Commodity	1976	1977 Value	% of Total	Percentage Increase (or decrease in 1977)
Exports total	15,690	19,717	100.0	25.7
Foodstuffs	236	200	1.0	(15.3)
Textiles	576	669	3.4	16.1
Chemicals	413	488	2.5	18.2
Nonmetallic mineral products	257	337	1.7	31.1
Metal products	2,900	3,305	16.8	14.0
Machinery and equipment	10,211	13,353	67.7	30.8
Others	1,097	1,365	6.9	24.4
Imports total	11,809	12,396	100.0	5.0
Foodstuffs	2,684	2,734	22.1	1.9
Raw materials	3,150	3,600	29.0	14.3
Mineral fuels	1,447	1,350	10.9	(6.7)
Chemicals	1,084	1,152	9.3	6.3
Machinery and equipment	2,252	2,369	19.1	5.2
Others	1,192	1,191	9.6	(0.1)
U.S. trade deficit with Japan	3,881	7,321		88.6

Source: Compiled by the author based on data from Japan External Trade Organization, White Paper on International Trade of Japan, 1977 (Tokyo: JETRO, 1977) and data provided by the Consulate General of Japan in New York City.

problems confronting U.S. companies and to act on complaints by
U.S. companies against Japanese nontariff barriers

The full impact of the above measures remains to be seen.
However, the Japanese government realizes that unless Japan's trade
surplus is cut drastically, it will be very difficult to stop the surge
of protectionism in the United States and in other countries.

The Alleged and Proven Dumping Practices of Japanese Firms

The dumping practices of Japanese firms have been widely
publicized as a result of complaints from U.S. manufacturers and
labor unions, and of many investigations carried out by the U.S.
government and the EEC. A senior official at the U.S. International
Trade Commission told the author that investigations of 47 cases
involving less than fair value imports from Japan were made between
April 1964 and April 1976.

The following is the normal procedure for a dumping investigation in the United States. Upon receiving a complaint, or upon his
own initiation, the secretary of the treasury has the authority, under
the Antidumping Act of 1921, to determine whether a class or kind
of foreign merchandise is being sold or is likely to be sold in the
United States at "less than fair value," which generally means at
prices less than those charged in the country of origin. If the secretary makes an affirmative determination, he refers the case to the
U.S. International Trade Commission, which has three months to
decide whether U.S. industry has been injured. If injury is found,
then antidumping duties can be imposed.

One of the more recent Japanese dumping cases involved steel
imports from Japan. In March 1977, the Treasury Department began
its investigations. Almost a year later, in February 1978, the U.S.
International Trade Commission ruled that Japanese trading companies and steelmakers were engaging in unfair competition in the
United States.[15]

In January 1978, the Treasury Department also announced a
"trigger price mechanism" plan to curb cheap imports of foreign
steel. This plan took effect in February 1978. The plan sets mini-
mum prices below which imported steel could "trigger" a Treasury
investigation to determine whether the steel had been sold at less
than fair value, which could lead to antidumping duties on the imports.
In March 1978, the Treasury announced an extended trigger price
plan, which brought more than 90 percent of imported steel under
the mechanism.[16]

As a result of the trigger price plan, steel imports from Japan are likely to decline in 1978. A leading spokesman for U.S. steel importers estimated pessimistically that steel imports in 1978 could plunge to about half the level of 1977.[17]

Devaluation of the U.S. Dollar

The value of the U.S. dollar has declined sharply against the Japanese yen and other major European currencies in recent months. For example, as shown in Table 3.3, the monthly closing exchange rate in units of yen per U.S. dollar declined by 29 percent between January 1977 and June 1978, and the monthly average exchange rate dropped by 26 percent during the same period. On July 24, 1978, the value of U.S. dollar fell below ¥200 in Tokyo for the first time since the end of World War II.[18] Further appreciation of the yen is considered likely unless the U.S. trade deficit can be reduced substantially, both by cutting oil imports and through the measures taken by the Japanese government.[19] These measures were discussed in the earlier sections of this chapter.

The revaluation of the yen has had the effect of making Japanese exports more expensive and less desirable to foreign buyers, and imports cheaper and more attractive to the Japanese. Many export-oriented companies, already experiencing thin profits, are finding margins further eroded. A recent survey of the leading 300 Japanese companies revealed an average 29 percent decline in profits between the April-September period of 1977 and the preceding six months from October 1976 to March 1977. Bankruptcies are also increasing. From an average 8,285 cases per year in the fiscal years 1971 through 1973, it soared to 16,606 cases in the fiscal year 1976 and 17,987 cases in fiscal year 1977. The unpaid liabilities of those firms that went bankrupt in the fiscal year 1977 were about ¥3.235 billion.[20]

The rise in the yen has also changed the corporate strategies of many Japanese firms and foreign-owned subsidiaries in Japan. Those companies that suffered from revaluation of the yen were trying to become more competitive in nonprice areas such as quality and services. A number of these companies had also tried to persuade their foreign customers to accept sales contracts that were denominated in yen.

A survey by Business Asia also found that many Japanese companies that imported foreign goods were not passing on to customers the gains from cheaper imports and currency translations. Instead, these companies used the opportunities to increase their spending on research and development, foreign investment, and advertising.[21]

TABLE 3.3: Monthly Exchange Rate of the Yen,
January 1977 to June 1978

| Month | Monthly Closing | | Monthly Average | |
	Exchange Rate[a]	% Devaluation (-) or Revaluation (+) of U.S. Dollar from Previous Month	Exchange Rate[b]	% Devaluation (-) or Revaluation (+) of U.S. Dollar from Previous Month
1977				
January	289.30		291.08	
February	282.70	-2.28	285.07	-2.06
March	277.50	-1.84	280.57	-1.58
April	277.10	-0.14	275.12	-1.94
May	277.30	+0.07	277.62	+0.91
June	267.70	-3.46	272.98	-1.67
July	266.00	-0.64	264.82	-2.99
August	267.30	+0.49	266.64	+0.69
September	265.45	-0.69	267.04	+0.15
October	250.60	-5.59	255.07	-4.48
November	245.70	-1.96	244.82	-4.02
December	240.00	-2.32	241.28	-1.45
1978				
January	241.40	+0.58	241.13	-0.06
February	238.70	-1.12	240.28	-0.35
March	222.40	-6.83	231.51	-3.65
April	222.90	+0.22	221.68	-4.25
May	223.40	+0.22	226.40	+2.13
June	204.70	-8.37	214.34	-5.33
Devaluation of U.S. dollar (from January 1977 to June 1978)		-29.24		-26.36

[a] This is the rate on the last day of a given month.
[b] This is the simple average of the daily rates for the month.
Note: All exchange rates are in units of yen per U.S. dollar.
Source: International Monetary Fund, International Financial
Statistics (Washington, D.C.: IMF, various issues).

SUMMARY

The essential characteristics of the Japanese business environment and the U.S.-Japanese bilateral economic issues were discussed in this chapter. We have observed that there have recently been many changes in the Japanese environment and in the bilateral relationship between the two countries. Some of these changes may have significant strategic implications for MNCs in the United States and in other countries.

Since the early part of the 1960s, the Japanese government has taken steps to liberalize its trade with other countries. Recent measures taken by Japan to narrow the trade gap with the United States are very encouraging. However, unless Japan manages to reduce her huge trade surplus in the near future, more trade concessions from the Japanese can be expected.

Another major development is the trend toward tightening the antitrust legislation in the United States and Japan. If an antitrust pact is signed by the two countries, it may create new problems for U.S. firms investing in Japan and for Japanese companies doing business in the United States. This is because any violation of antitrust laws in one country could have adverse effects on subsidiaries in the other country. However, many U.S. and European MNCs may benefit, in one respect, from the enforcement of Japanese antimonopoly laws because enforcement could lead to the breakup of several large Japanese firms, thus reducing their competitive edge in international markets.

The devaluation of the U.S. dollar and mounting U.S. antidumping investigations have caused major changes in Japanese business strategies. As described earlier, more and more Japanese firms are employing nonprice strategies than ever before. Moreover, significant increases of Japanese investments in North America and Western Europe can be expected. As a result, international transfer pricing will become a more important and delicate issue in the future for Japanese MNCs.

NOTES

1. Some information presented in this section can also be found in Taizo Hayashi, Guide to Japanese Taxes 1977-78 (Tokyo: Zaikei Shōhō sha, 1977); Ernst & Ernst, A Digest of Principal Taxes in Japan (New York: Ernst & Ernst, 1975); Price Waterhouse, Corporate Taxes in 80 Countries (New York: Price Waterhouse, 1978); and Haskins & Sells, Taxation in Japan (New York: Haskin & Sells, 1977).

2. Haskins & Sells, op. cit., p. 10.

3. Price Waterhouse, op. cit., pp. 150-51.

4. Haruko Fukuda, Japan and World Trade: The Years Ahead (Lexington, Mass.: Lexington Books, 1973), pp. 77-78.

5. Wall Street Journal, March 3, 1978.

6. A National Profile, International Business Series on Japan (New York: Ernst and Ernst, 1970), p. 19.

7. Business International, July 8, 1977.

8. Jeffrey S. Arpan, International Intracorporate Pricing: Non-American Systems and Views (New York: Praeger, 1972), p. 84.

9. M. Y. Yoshino, Japan's Multinational Enterprises (Cambridge, Mass.: Harvard University Press, 1976), pp. 148-150.

10. American Institute of Certified Public Accountants (AICPA), "Consolidated Financial Statements," Accounting Research Bulletin, no. 51 (New York: 1959).

11. The Business Accounting Deliberation Board, Renketsu Zaimu-shoyō no Seido-ka ni Kansuru Iken-sho (Opinion on the Systematization of Consolidated Financial Statements) (Tokyo, Business Accounting Principles Board, 1975). Also quoted in Robert J. Ballon, Iwao Tomita, and Hajime Usami, Financial Reporting in Japan (Tokyo: Kodansha International, 1976), p. 246.

12. The Ministry of Finance of Japan, Renketsu Zaimusyohyō Kisoku (Rules for Preparing Consolidated Financial Statements) (Tokyo: Ministry of Finance, 1976).

13. See "Japan's Accounting Shake-up," Business Week, April 25, 1977, p. 114.

14. Louis Kraar, "Japan's Great Buying Offensive," Fortune, April 24, 1978, pp. 42-44. The U.S. deficit with Japan in the first six months of 1978 was $6.32 billion, nearly double that of the same period in 1977. See details in Wall Street Journal, July 28, 1978.

15. Wall Street Journal, February 10, 1978.

16. Ibid., March 24, 1978.

17. Ibid., January 5, 1978.

18. Ibid., July 25, 1978.

19. The total trade deficit of the United States for the first half of 1978 stood at $16.37 billion, which is 42 percent higher than for the same period in 1977.

20. See "The Japanese Economy Today and U.S.-Japan Economic Relations," Business Week, July 24, 1978, p. 18.

21. Business Asia, April 21, 1978.

4

RESEARCH DESIGN
AND METHODOLOGY

As described in Chapter 1, data were gathered for this study through the use of several research methods, including a review of the literature, a questionnaire survey, and interviews and discussions with partners of international accounting firms and experienced professors. This chapter explains the details of research design and methodology used. A substantial amount of the discussion will be devoted to the questionnaire survey, which was the backbone of the research.

SEARCH OF THE LITERATURE

All relevant literature written in the English language that could be located was read and analyzed. Although many readings were done on side issues, the topics specifically searched out included the following:

Domestic transfer pricing in the United States and other countries
International transfer pricing
Japanese business environment to the extent that it affects the transfer pricing practices of large industrial companies
Recent developments in U.S.-Japanese bilateral trade, devaluation of the U.S. dollar against the Japanese yen, and other related issues
Major U.S. tax legislation and other regulations having an impact upon the transfer pricing practices of large industrial companies

Details of the first two areas were reported in Chapter 2 and the areas related to the Japanese environment and U.S.-Japanese bilateral issues were discussed in Chapter 3. Major features of U.S. tax legislation and regulations will be outlined in Chapters 5 and 6.

The search of literature in these areas was done to accomplish the following objectives:

To build a solid conceptual foundation needed for the study and to determine the extent of research that had been done in the areas of domestic and international transfer pricing

To find the key environmental variables normally considered by MNCs in formulating their international transfer pricing policies

To understand the business environments in the United States and Japan, which would help the author interpret similarities and differences between the U.S. and Japanese transfer pricing practices

QUESTIONNAIRE SURVEY

A questionnaire survey was used to gather the latest empirical information on some important transfer pricing practices among large industrial corporations in the United States and Japan. This section will describe the populations and the implementation of both the pilot study and the full-scale study.

Definition of Populations

Many lists and directories were considered in determining the populations for this study. Finally, it was decided to use three directories to define the two national populations. These were the 1976 Fortune directories of the 500 largest and the second 500 largest U.S. industrial corporations,[1] and the President Directory 1976 of the 1,121 leading mining and manufacturing corporations in Japan.[2] These directories were selected not only because they were more complete and updated than other sources at the time the survey was conducted, but also because the U.S. and Japanese companies included in these directories were more comparable. The President directory of Japanese firms included only the largest mining and manufacturing corporations in Japan, and the Fortune directories included only companies that derived more than 50 percent of their revenue from manufacturing and/or mining. Also, the companies included in both directories were listed on the stock exchanges in each respective country.

After selecting the directories, another question was how to determine the populations of both groups to be surveyed. It was decided that the two populations defined must be big enough so that large samples could be drawn, and yet the populations were to be comparable in terms of size. Both directories had the data on sales, total assets, and number of employees for all corporations listed. Sales data were used as the measure of size to define the populations of the two national groups mainly because sales volume was used by both directories to provide the major rankings of U.S. or Japanese industrial firms.

The largest and smallest firms of the two directories and their sales figures are as follows:

Rank	Sales (thousands of U.S. dollars)
Fortune directories	
1 Exxon	44,864,824
1,000 Electronic Memories and Magnetics	92,198
President directories	
1 Nippon Steel	7,623,417
1,121 Yutaka Shoyu	2,043

It can be seen that the range of sales of firms listed in the above directories is quite different. In order to have the two populations comparable in terms of sales, an upper limit and a lower limit of sales dollars for firms in each directory to be included in the U.S. and Japanese populations were determined as follows:

The upper limit: Sales dollars of the No. 1 firm in terms of sales rank in the President directories, which was 7.623 million in U.S. dollars.

The lower limit: Sales of the No. 1,000 firm in terms of sales rank in the Fortune directories, which was 92 million in U.S. dollars.

By this definition, 986 U.S. firms in the Fortune directory (from No. 15 to No. 1,000 in terms of sales rank) were defined as the population of the large U.S. industrial firms. In the President directory, 401 Japanese firms (from No. 1 to No. 401 in terms of sales rank) were defined as the population of the large Japanese industrial firms.

Pilot Study

A pilot study was launched in February and March of 1977 to test the feasibility of a full-scale study and to serve the following purposes:

To discover whether there were ambiguities and occurrences of bias resulting from the wording of the cover letters and questionnaires.

To get objective response rates so that sample sizes for the full-scale study could be determined.

To determine whether Japanese firms have difficulty in answering an English language questionnaire. If so, a Japanese questionnaire or a bilingual questionnaire would be needed.

To test the effect of an incentive provided in the survey. The incentive was an offer to provide a copy of the summary report to any firm that responded and wished to have a copy of the report.

A sample of 30 firms was chosen from each of the two national populations for the pilot study using a systematic sampling method.[3] On February 15, 1977, copies of the pilot study questionnaire were sent to those firms along with the cover letters. The letters to U.S. firms were addressed to the controller, treasurer, financial vice-president, or secretary, and stamped return envelopes were provided. The letters to Japanese firms were sent to the presidents of the companies because names of the financial executives were not available at the time this study was undertaken.

The pilot study questionnaire included four sections. Section 1 contained questions on transfer pricing methods currently used by the company. Section 2 asked for opinions as to the importance of 15 environmental variables to be considered when the company formulated its international transfer pricing policies. Section 3 requested information on some policy issues related to transfer pricing. Section 4 asked for general information about the corporation.

Follow-up letters were sent out in March 1977. The response rates, as shown in Table 4.1, were considered to be reasonably good, given the confidential nature of the information requested. The rate of response of U.S. firms was 47 percent whereas the response rate of Japanese companies was 43 percent. The overall response rate to the pilot study was 45 percent of the 60 firms on the mailing list.

The results from the pilot study indicated that a full-scale study based on larger samples was feasible and that Japanese firms did not have undue difficulty in answering the English questionnaire.

TABLE 4.1: Responses to the Pilot Study

	U.S. Companies	Japanese Companies	Total
No. of questionnaires sent	30	30	60
No. of responses:			
Early responses	11	6	17
Responses to follow-up letters	3	7	10
Total responses	14	13	27
Overall response rates	47%	43%	45%

Source: Compiled by the author.

Seven of the 14 U.S. firms that responded to the pilot study asked for copies of the summary report. Only two of the 13 Japanese respondents did the same. If the offer of the summary report was effective at all, evidently it was more of an incentive for U.S. firms than for Japanese firms. This incentive was again used in the full-scale study to offer maximum encouragement for filling out the questionnaire.

The pilot study questionnaire and the results of the pilot study were reviewed by a number of experienced professors and public accountants, including some in other countries. The questionnaire was then revised and finalized in April 1977. The major revisions of each of the four sections of the questionnaire included the following:

In Section 1 ("Transfer Pricing Methods Currently Used"), two more questions were added. One question asked the firms that did not use transfer price to indicate the main reason for not using it. The other asked the firms to identify the most important (or dominant) methods for their domestic transfers and international transfers because the use of more than one transfer price was common among the respondents of the pilot study.

In Section 2, the list of environmental variables was expanded from 15 to 20.

In Section 3, one question was added in the hope of identifying the dominant corporate objectives of the transfer pricing system.

In Section 4, additional questions were asked in order to find out more general information about the respondents. This information included total revenue, the number of countries in which the company had foreign subsidiaries, the country that accounted for the greatest amount of the parent company's exports to or imports from foreign subsidiaries. It was believed that such changes would permit the collection of more complete data on the transfer pricing practices of respondents.

Full-Scale Study

Based on the experience of the pilot study, it was decided to survey 300 U.S. firms and the remaining firms in the Japanese population (371 all together) that were not covered by the pilot study. Later it was found that the addresses of two Japanese firms could not be located. Therefore, the actual sample sizes of the full-scale study for U.S. and Japanese corporations were 300 and 369, respectively.

In April 1977, copies of the revised questionnaire, along with the cover letters, were sent to the 369 Japanese and 300 U.S. firms. None of these firms had participated in the pilot study. The U.S. firms were selected using a systematic sampling method. Follow-up letters and copies of the questionnaire were sent to the firms that had not yet responded by June 1, 1977.

The responses to the full-scale study are summarized in Table 4.2. Of the 300 questionnaires sent to U.S. firms, 154 responses were received, representing a response rate of 51 percent. Of the 369 questionnaires sent to Japanese firms, 112 responses were received, yielding a response rate of 30 percent. The overall response rate was 40 percent. The rates of usable responses from U.S. and Japanese firms were 48 percent and 28 percent, respectively, whereas the overall usable response rate was 37 percent.

A comparison between the responses to the pilot study and to the full-scale study shows that the response rate of U.S. firms in the full-scale study was four percentage points higher than that of the pilot study. In contrast, the response rate of Japanese firms in the full-scale study was 13 percentage points lower than that of the pilot study. The higher response rate of U.S. firms had not been expected by the researcher. The lower response rate of the Japanese firms in the full-scale study was probably caused by two events that happened after the pilot study was launched. First of all, the U.S. International Trade Commission (ITC) ruled unanimously in March 1977 that color television imports from Japan were injuring the U.S. industry. There was continuous publicity about this case until an agreement was reached between the U.S. and Japanese governments

TABLE 4.2: Responses to the Full-Scale Study

Questionnaire	U.S. Companies	Japanese Companies	Total
Sent	300	369	669
Returned usable	145	102	247
Returned unusable	9	10	19
Not returned	146	257	403
	300	369	669
Response rates	51%	30%	40%
Rates of usable responses	48%	28%	37%

Source: Compiled by the author.

to limit color television imports from Japan in May 1977. The second factor concerns consolidated financial statements. Prior to April 1, 1977, many large Japanese companies did not prepare consolidated statements and, as indicated in Chapter 3, transfer prices may have been abused in some instances. Because of these factors, some Japanese companies may have chosen not to respond to the full-scale study probing into their transfer pricing practices.

STATISTICAL METHODS USED FOR
INFERENCE IN THE STUDY

A number of statistical methods were used to test the seven hypotheses stated earlier in Chapter 1. Computer programs available in the SPSS package were used for the analysis.[4]

Hypotheses A-1 and A-2 deal with the relationships between the extent of application of cost-oriented or non-cost-oriented transfer prices among the respondent firms and their nationality. The chi-square test was used to detect the significant relationships between the nationality and the use of cost-oriented or non-cost-oriented transfer prices.[5]

Hypotheses B-1, B-2, B-3, and B-4 deal with the relationships between the size of the parent company and the extent of using cost-oriented transfer prices. Companies that used transfer prices to account for interdivisional transfers were grouped by total revenue categories and by the use or nonuse of cost-oriented transfer prices. The chi-square test was again used to detect any significant relationship between the size factor and the use or nonuse of cost-oriented transfer prices.

Hypothesis C-1 deals with the importance of 20 environmental variables normally considered by MNCs in formulating their international transfer pricing policies. A t test was used to detect the significant differences between the importance assigned by the U.S. firms and by the Japanese firms to each variable.[6]

To determine whether the rank orderings of the two national groups on all 20 variables were correlated, two rank order tests, the Kendall correlation coefficient and the Spearman correlation coefficient, were conducted.[7]

Hypotheses D-1 and D-2 deal with the relationships between the ratings of the 20 variables and the total revenue of the firm. Again, the chi-square test was used to detect the existence or nonexistence of any of the hypothesized relationships.

To find out whether there was significant nonresponse bias incorporated into the study for each of the two national groups, a comparison was made between the responses of early respondents and respondents to follow-up letters sent approximately six weeks after the initial mailing. Respondents to the follow-up letters were assumed to hold opinions substantially similar to nonrespondents.[8] The comparison was made for most survey questions by means of the chi-square test of homogeneity.

INTERVIEWS

Before drawing final conclusions, and to determine any possible discrepancies in the results from the questionnaire survey, the results of the full-scale study were reviewed by professors experienced in business research and by two partners of international accounting firms. These two partners had extensive experience working with international companies and had expressed interest in this research. After these professors and accountants read the results of the study, they were interviewed in their offices. Their observations and conclusions are reported in Chapter 6.

SUMMARY

The research design and methodology were described in this chapter. The review of literature not only helped the author build the solid conceptual foundation needed for this study but also enabled him to design an initial version of the questionnaire.

A questionnaire survey was implemented in two stages: the pilot study and the full-scale study. This survey was used to gather the empirical information needed to test the research hypotheses and to provide insight into the transfer pricing practices of large industrial companies in the United States and Japan. From the 669 questionnaires mailed for the full-scale study, 266 responses were received. Of these, there were 247 usable responses representing a usable response rate of 37 percent.

A number of statistical methods were used in this study. These included a t test, chi-square test, Spearman correlation coefficient, and Kendall correlation coefficient. Finally, several professors and two accounting partners were interviewed to validate the findings and results of this study.

Inasmuch as the details of the research methodology have been described in this chapter, the findings and analysis of the responses to the full-scale study will be discussed in Chapters 5 and 6.

NOTES

1. See "The Fortune Directory of the 500 Largest U.S. Industrial Corporations," Fortune, May 1976, pp. 316-43; and "The Fortune Directory of the Second 500 Largest U.S. Industrial Corporations," Fortune, June 1976, pp. 212-40.

2. "The 1,121 Leading Japanese Mining and Manufacturing Corporations," The President Directory 1976 (Tokyo: The Diamond-Time Co., 1976), pp. 28-52.

3. For an introduction to the systematic sampling method, see Taro Yamane, Elementary Sampling Theory (Englewood Cliffs, N.J.: Prentice-Hall, 1967), pp. 159-85.

4. Norman H. Nie et al., Statistical Package for the Social Sciences (New York: McGraw-Hill, 1975).

5. For an explanation of the chi-square test, see, for example, W. J. Conoven, Practical Nonparametric Statistics (New York: John Wiley and Sons, 1971), pp. 140-201.

6. For a good introduction to the t test of significance, see Nie et al., op. cit., pp. 267-71.

7. Sidney Siegal, Nonparametric Statistics for the Behavioural Sciences (New York: McGraw-Hill, 1956), pp. 202-23.

8. For evidence supporting the validity of this test, see A. N. Oppenheim, Questionnaire Design and Attitude Measurement (New York: Basic Books, 1966), p. 34.

5

FINDINGS AND ANALYSIS:
CHARACTERISTICS AND
TRANSFER PRICING METHODS
OF RESPONDENT FIRMS

Major findings and results of the analysis are presented in Chapters 5 and 6. This chapter describes some important characteristics of the respondent firms and their transfer pricing methods. Findings and analysis concerning environmental variables and other issues will be reported in the next chapter.

This chapter is divided into three sections. In the first section, the major characteristics of respondent firms are described. The second section presents the extent of usage of transfer prices among U.S. and Japanese companies and the types of transfer prices used by these companies to account for their domestic and international interdivisional transfers. The third section reports the results of the tests of hypotheses related to transfer pricing methods (hypotheses A-1, A-2, B-1, B-2, B-3, and B-4).

SOME CHARACTERISTICS OF THE RESPONDENT FIRMS

The characteristics of the respondent firms described in this section include industrial classification, total revenue, number of foreign subsidiaries, exports to and imports from foreign subsidiaries, and the magnitude of interdivisional transfers. All of these data were collected through the questionnaire survey.

Industrial Classification

Table 5.1 shows the industrial classification of those U.S. and Japanese companies that responded to the survey. The industries

TABLE 5.1: Industrial Classification of the Respondent Firms

Industry Code	Industry	United States		Japan	
		Number of Firms	Percent of Total	Number of Firms	Percent of Total
10	Mining, crude oil production	3	2.1	0	0
20	Food	19	13.1	10	9.8
21	Tobacco	1	0.7	0	0
22	Textiles, vinyl flooring	7	4.8	3	2.9
23	Apparel	2	1.4	0	0
25	Furniture	2	1.4	1	1.0
26	Paper, fiber, and wood products	5	3.4	3	2.9
27	Publishing, printing	4	2.8	2	2.0
28	Chemicals	7	4.8	16	15.7
29	Petroleum refining	8	5.5	4	3.9
30	Rubber, plastic products	2	1.4	3	2.9
32	Glass, concrete, abrasives, gypsum	5	3.4	7	6.9
33	Metal manufacturing	9	6.2	13	12.7
34	Metal products	14	9.7	5	4.9

(continued)

49

Table 5. 1 (continued)

Industry Code	Industry	United States		Japan	
		Number of Firms	Percent of Total	Number of Firms	Percent of Total
36	Electronics, appliances	15	10.3	3	2.9
37	Shipbuilding, railroad, and transportation equipment	5	3.4	10	9.8
38	Measuring, scientific, photographic equipment	7	4.8	3	2.9
40	Motor vehicles	4	2.8	2	2.0
41	Aerospace	4	2.8	0	0
42	Pharmaceuticsls	2	1.4	2	2.0
43	Soaps, cosmetics	2	1.4	0	0
44	Office equipment (includes computers)	5	3.4	1	1.0
45	Industrial and farm equipment	7	4.8	11	10.8
47	Musical instruments, toys, sporting goods	0	0	1	1.0
49	Beverages	2	1.4	2	2.0
	Nonclassifiable	4	2.8	0	0
		145	100.0	102	100.0

Source: Compiled by the author.

50

were classified by a two-digit industrial code standing for the industry to which a company belongs. These industrial codes were used in the _Fortune_ directories and were based primarily on the categories established by the U.S. Office of Management and Budget.

As shown in the table, these companies represent a large variety of industries. Of the 145 U.S. respondent firms, four were not classifiable because there was not enough information regarding their industries. The rest of the firms came from 24 different industries. Five industries accounted for about 45 percent of the U.S. respondent firms. These were food, 13.1 percent; electronics and appliances, 10.3 percent; metal products, 9.7 percent; metal manufacturing, 6.2 percent; and petroleum refining, 5.5 percent.

The 102 Japanese respondent companies represent 20 industries. The five major industries, which accounted for about 59 percent of the respondent firms, were chemicals, 15.7 percent; metal manufacturing, 12.7 percent; industrial and farm equipment, 10.8 percent; food, 9.8 percent; and shipbuilding, railroad, and transportation equipment, 9.8 percent.

Total Revenue in 1976

The distribution of total revenues of U.S. and Japanese respondent firms is shown in Table 5.2. In percentage terms, there were

TABLE 5.2: Total Revenues of the Respondent Firms

Total Revenue in 1976	United States		Japan	
	Number of Firms	Percent of Total	Number of Firms	Percent of Total
Less than U.S. $100 million	6	4.2	11	10.8
U.S. $100 million to $200 million	35	24.1	19	18.6
U.S. $200 million to $400 million	36	24.8	30	29.4
U.S. $400 million to $1,000 million	36	24.8	27	26.5
Above U.S. $1,000 million	32	22.1	15	14.7
Total	145	100.0	102	100.0

Source: Compiled by the author.

more U.S. respondents in the second group with total revenue from
$100 million to $200 million, and in the last group with revenues
above $1,000 million. The percentages of Japanese firms in the
other three groups were higher. However, total revenues for U.S.
and Japanese firms in the sample were roughly comparable.

Number of Foreign Countries in which the Respondent Firms Have Subsidiaries

As shown in Table 5.3, 27.5 percent of the U.S. firms and
26.5 percent of the Japanese companies had no subsidiaries in foreign
countries. Hence, these firms were not MNCs according to the
definition of a multinational company used in this study. The remainder could be classified as multinational firms. A majority of the
Japanese MNCs had subsidiaries in one to five foreign countries
whereas many U.S. MNCs (29.7 percent) had subsidiaries in more
than 10 foreign countries. Relatively, the scale of U.S. MNC's
operations was broader than that of Japanese MNCs.

Exports to Foreign Subsidiaries

As presented in Table 5.4, 99 U.S. and 69 Japanese companies
indicated that they exported to foreign subsidiaries. Overall, the

TABLE 5.3: Number of Foreign Countries in Which
the Respondent Firms Had Subsidiaries

Number of Countries	United States		Japan	
	Number of Firms	Percent of Total	Number of Firms	Percent of Total
None	40	27.5	27	26.5
Multinationals:				
1 to 5 countries	43	29.7	55	53.9
6 to 10 countries	19	13.1	14	13.7
More than 10 countries	43	29.7	6	5.9
Total	145	100.0	102	100.0

Source: Compiled by the author.

TABLE 5.4: Exports to Foreign Subsidiaries
            by Respondent Firms

Amount of Exports	United States		Japan	
	Number of Firms	Percent of Total	Number of Firms	Percent of Total
Less than U.S. $0.5 million	16	16.2	21	30.4
U.S. $0.5 million to $1 million	7	7.1	7	10.2
U.S. $1 million to $10 million	42	42.4	16	23.2
U.S. $10 million to $50 million	19	19.2	12	17.4
Above U.S. $50 million	15	15.1	13	18.8
Total	99	100.0	69	100.0

Source: Compiled by the author.

amounts of exports to foreign subsidiaries of Japanese firms were
smaller than those of the U.S. companies. The noticeable differences
between the two national groups were in the first category (less than
$0.5 million) and the third category ($1 million to $10 million). More
than 30 percent of the Japanese firms were in the first category,
whereas about 42 percent of the U.S. firms were in the third category.

The countries that accounted for the greatest amount of exports
to foreign subsidiaries by U.S. firms are shown in Table 5.5. As
indicated in that table, 35 U.S. companies (43.8 percent) named
Canada as the country to which they exported the greatest amount to
their subsidiaries. Next to Canada was the United Kingdom, named
by 12 U.S. companies. The German Federal Republic was mentioned
by 10 companies. These correspond to the fact that Canada, the
United Kingdom, and West Germany were the three countries where
U.S. businesses had most of their direct foreign investments in 1976.
U.S. investments in these three countries accounted for 43.7 percent
of all U.S. direct foreign investments as of the end of 1976.[1]

Table 5.6 shows the countries that accounted for the greatest
amount of exports to foreign subsidiaries of 63 Japanese companies.
More than half of the Japanese firms named the United States as the
country to which they had the greatest amount of exports to their
subsidiaries. The next two most important countries were Taiwan

TABLE 5.5: Countries Accounting for the Greatest
Dollar Amount of Exports to Foreign
Subsidiaries by U.S. Firms

Countries Exported to	Number of Firms	Percent of Total
Canada	35	43.8
United Kingdom	12	15.0
Federal Republic of Germany	10	12.5
Belgium	4	5.0
Netherlands	4	5.0
Switzerland	3	3.7
Mexico	2	2.5
Venezuela	2	2.5
Taiwan	1	1.3
Indonesia	1	1.3
France	1	1.3
Hong Kong	1	1.3
Japan	1	1.3
Malta	1	1.3
Puerto Rico	1	1.3
Sweden	1	1.3
Total	80*	100.0

*The other 19 U.S. companies did not provide names of countries, presumably because these were considered confidential or because their exports to foreign subsidiaries were negligible.
Source: Compiled by the author.

and South Korea, which were named by eight (12.7 percent) and six (9.5 percent) Japanese companies, respectively.

Imports from Foreign Subsidiaries

As shown in Table 5.7, 91 U.S. companies and 59 Japanese companies indicated that they imported products from the foreign subsidiaries. In terms of percentages, there were more U.S. firms in the first category, with imports less than $0.5 million, and the last category, with imports above $50 million. The percentages of Japanese firms in the other three categories were slightly higher.

Table 5.8 shows the countries of origin of imports into the United States for products made by foreign subsidiaries of U.S. firms. According to the table, Canada was ranked top among all the countries, followed by the United Kingdom, Singapore, and Taiwan.

As shown in Table 5.9, 21 Japanese firms (42 percent) named the United States as the country from which the greatest amount of their imports from foreign subsidiaries originated. This was followed by South Korea, Australia, Malaysia, and the German Federal Republic.

TABLE 5.6: Countries Accounting for the Greatest
Dollar Amount of Exports to Foreign
Subsidiaries by Japanese Firms

Countries Exported to	Number of Firms	Percent of Total
United States	33	52.4
Taiwan	8	12.7
South Korea	6	9.5
Thailand	3	4.7
Hong Kong	2	3.2
Federal Republic of Germany	2	3.1
Canada	1	1.6
Indonesia	1	1.6
Brazil	1	1.6
Singapore	1	1.6
Philippines	1	1.6
Belgium	1	1.6
Australia	1	1.6
Salvador	1	1.6
USSR	1	1.6
Total	63*	100.0

*The other six Japanese corporations did not provide names of countries, presumably because these names were considered confidential or their exports to foreign subsidiaries were negligible.

Source: Compiled by the author.

TABLE 5.7: Imports from Foreign Subsidiaries
by the Respondent Firms

Amounts of Imports	United States		Japan	
	Number of Firms	Percent of Total	Number of Firms	Percent of Total
Less than U.S. $0.5 million	48	52.7	27	45.7
U.S. $0.5 million to $1 million	8	8.8	7	11.9
U.S. $1 million to $10 million	22	24.2	17	28.8
U.S. $10 million to $50 million	9	9.9	7	11.9
Above U.S. $50 million	4	4.4	1	1.7
Total	91	100.0	59	100.0

Source: Compiled by the author.

Percentages of Interdivisional Transfers
to Total Revenue

As shown in Table 5.10, the percentages of interdivisional
transfers to total revenue of the U.S. firms were comparable to
those of the Japanese firms. More than one-third of both the responding U.S. and Japanese firms had intracompany transfers of less than
5 percent of their total revenues.

An Evaluation

From the characteristics described above it may be seen that
respondent firms in the two national groups were comparable in
terms of total revenue, volume of exports to and imports from foreign
subsidiaries, and percentage of interdivisional transfers to total
revenue. However, the scale of U.S. MNCs' operations was some-

what broader than that of Japanese MNCs. Companies in the United States tended to trade more with their subsidiaries in Canada, the United Kingdom, and the German Federal Republic than with subsidiaries in other countries, whereas Japanese companies traded heavily with their U.S. subsidiaries.

TABLE 5.8: Countries Where Greatest Dollar Volume of Imports from U.S. Subsidiaries Originated

Countries Imported from	Number of Firms	Percent of Total
Canada	23	34.9
United Kingdom	13	19.7
Singapore	4	6.1
Taiwan	4	6.1
Hong Kong	3	4.6
Mexico	3	4.6
German Federal Republic	3	4.5
France	2	3.0
Japan	2	3.0
Iran	1	1.5
Switzerland	1	1.5
Brazil	1	1.5
Netherlands	1	1.5
Philippines	1	1.5
Belgium	1	1.5
Suriname	1	1.5
Algeria	1	1.5
Portugal	1	1.5
Total	66*	100.0

*Twenty-five U.S. firms did not provide names of countries, presumably because these names were considered confidential or their imports from foreign subsidiaries were negligible.

Source: Compiled by the author.

TABLE 5.9: Countries Where Greatest Dollar Volume
of Imports from Japanese Subsidiaries
Originated

Countries Imported from	Number of Firms	Percent of Total
United States	21	42.0
South Korea	6	12.0
Australia	4	8.0
Malaysia	4	8.0
German Federal Republic	4	8.0
United Kingdom	2	4.0
Taiwan	2	4.0
Thailand	2	4.0
Canada	1	2.0
Singapore	1	2.0
New Zealand	1	2.0
Zaire	1	2.0
Peru	1	2.0
Total	50*	100.0

*Nine Japanese companies did not provide names of countries, because either these names were considered confidential or their imports from foreign subsidiaries were negligible.

Source: Compiled by the author.

TABLE 5.10: Interdivisional Transfers as Percentages
of Total Revenues of Respondent Firms

Percentage of Transfers to Total Revenues	United States		Japan	
	Number of Firms	Percent of Total	Number of Firms	Percent of Total
Less than 5 percent	50	37.6	30	34.9
5 to 10 percent	34	25.6	24	27.9
10.1 to 20 percent	20	15.0	13	15.1
20.1 to 40 percent	19	14.3	13	15.1
Above 40 percent	10	7.5	6	7.0
	133*	100.0	86*	100.0

*Twelve U.S. firms and fifteen Japanese firms declined to provide information on the percentages of interdivisional transfers.

Source: Compiled by the author.

TRANSFER PRICING METHODS

The Use of Transfer Prices

Table 5.11 shows that 133 U.S. firms (or 91.7 percent of the U.S. respondents) and 74 Japanese firms (or 72.5 percent of the Japanese respondents) make use of transfer prices. Hence, the use of transfer prices among large U.S. industrial firms is more extensive than in large Japanese industrial firms.

The use of transfer prices among large industrial firms has increased significantly over the past 20 years. When Stone studied this subject, the percentage of pricing companies in his sample was only 71 percent.[2] In the present study, the percentage of transfer pricing companies jumped to 91.7 percent. This reflects the fact that the operations of large industrial firms are becoming more diversified and decentralized than they were formerly.

Table 5.12 summarizes the reasons provided by a number of companies for not using transfer prices. Insignificant volume of interdivisional transfers was cited by a majority of U.S. and Japanese firms and one U.S. company feared that a transfer pricing system might be too complicated to operate. One Japanese petroleum firm had previously used a transfer price but stopped using it because it was too complicated to update transfer prices to meet the changes in material costs, exchange rates, and other economic variables.

TABLE 5.11: The Use and Nonuse of Transfer Prices Among the Respondent Firms

	United States		Japan	
	Number of Firms	Percent of Total	Number of Firms	Percent of Total
Users	133	91.7	74	72.5
Nonusers	12	8.3	28	27.5
Total	145	100.0	102	100.0

Source: Compiled by the author.

TABLE 5.12: Reasons Given by Nonusers for Not
Using Transfer Prices

	United States		Japan	
Reasons	Number of Firms	Percent of Total	Number of Firms	Percent of Total
Volume of transfer insignificant	10	77	19	66
Transfer pricing system too complicated	1	8	6	21
Used transfer prices before but stopped for some reasons	0	0	1	3
Other reasons	2	15	3	10
Total	13*	100	29*	100

*One U.S. firm and one Japanese company reported two
reasons for not using transfer prices.
Source: Compiled by the author.

Transfer Prices for Domestic Transfer

Table 5.13 shows the transfer prices reported as used by 133
U.S. and 73 Japanese pricing companies to account for their domestic
interdivisional transfers. Table 5.14 presents the dominant domestic
prices used by the same 133 U.S. and 73 Japanese companies. If a
company reported that it used only one transfer price for domestic
transfers, that price was considered to be the dominant transfer
price of the company. If a firm reported that it used more than one
transfer price for domestic transfers, that firm was asked to name
the dominant (or most important) domestic transfer price used in
the firm. These responses were used for Table 5.14.

Tables 5.13 and 5.14 show that the more popular domestic
transfer pricing methods used by U.S. firms were market price,
full production cost-plus, negotiated price, and standard full production cost. The more widely used methods among Japanese firms
were full-production cost-plus, negotiated price, market price,
market price less selling expenses, and standard full-production
cost.

TABLE 5.13: Transfer Pricing Methods Used by the
Respondent Firms for Domestic Transfers

Pricing Methods	United States		Japan	
	Number of Firms	Percent of Total	Number of Firms	Percent of Total
Cost-oriented methods:				
Actual variable cost of production	0	0	0	0
Actual full-production cost	21	9.0	11	9.2
Standard variable cost of production	7	3.0	1	0.8
Standard full-production cost	39	16.9	18	15.1
Actual variable production cost plus a lump-sum subsidy	2	0.9	1	0.9
Full-production cost (actual or standard) plus some allowance for profit	44	19.0	24	20.2
Other cost-oriented methods	4	1.7	0	0
Subtotal for cost-oriented methods	117	50.4	55	46.2
Non-cost-oriented methods:				
Market price	50	21.6	21	17.7
Market price less selling expenses	19	8.2	19	16.0
Negotiated price	42	18.1	23	19.3
Mathematical programming price	0	0	1	0.8
Other non-cost-oriented methods	4	1.7	0	0
Subtotal for non-cost-oriented methods	115	49.6	64	53.8
Total—all methods	232	100.0	119	100.0

Source: Compiled by the author.

TABLE 5.14: The Dominant Transfer Pricing Methods Used
by Respondent Firms for Domestic Transfers

Dominant Transfer Pricing Methods[a]	United States		Japan	
	Number of Firms	Percent of Total	Number of Firms	Percent of Total
Cost-oriented methods:				
Actual variable cost of production	0	0	0	0
Actual full-production cost	11	8.3	8	10.9
Standard variable cost of production	2	1.5	1	1.4
Standard full-production cost	27	20.3	13	17.8
Actual variable production cost plus a lump-sum subsidy	1	0.7	1	1.4
Full-production cost (actual or standard) plus some allowance for profit	32	24.1	11	15.1
Other cost-oriented methods	1	1.5	0	0
Subtotal for cost-oriented method	75	56.4	34	46.6
Non-cost-oriented methods:				
Market price	27	20.3	12	16.4
Market price less selling expenses	11	8.3	17	23.3
Negotiated price	17	12.8	10	13.7
Mathematical programming price	0	0	0	0
Other non-cost-oriented methods	3	2.2	0	0
Subtotal for non-cost-oriented methods	58	43.6	39	53.4
Total—all methods	133	100.0	73[b]	100.0

[a]Dominant transfer pricing method is the single or most important transfer pricing method used by the firm to account for domestic interdivisional transfers.

[b]One Japanese pricing company has an international transfer price, but not a domestic transfer price.

Source: Compiled by the author.

At first, one may get the impression by looking at Table 5.13 that the total number of domestic transfer pricing methods used by either U.S. firms or Japanese firms was about equally divided between the cost-oriented methods and non-cost-oriented methods. However, when one looks at Table 5.14, it becomes obvious that in the United States, cost-oriented methods were used more often than non-cost-oriented methods for the dominant domestic transfer prices. There was no such shift of orientation in Japan.

A comparison between the percentages of various methods in Tables 5.13 and 5.14 shows that full-production cost-plus was used more often in the United States as the dominant domestic transfer price, whereas in Japan market price less selling expenses was used more frequently as the dominant domestic transfer price. Proportionally, negotiated price was used less frequently by both national groups as dominant transfer prices.

At this point, it is difficult to say whether or not the difference between the orientations of domestic transfer prices used by the two national groups is significant. But, the statistical tests of hypotheses A-1 and A-2 will help us in drawing such conclusions. These statistical tests and their results will be discussed later in this chapter.

Table 5.15 shows that many Japanese and U.S. firms used more than one domestic transfer price. Thirty U.S. and nineteen Japanese companies used dual transfer prices. One U.S. firm used as many as six transfer pricing methods.

TABLE 5.15: Number of Domestic Transfer Pricing Methods Used by the Respondent Firms

Number of Methods Used	Number of Companies	Percent of Total	Number of Companies	Percent of Total
One	74	55.6	42	57.6
Two	30	22.6	19	26.0
Three	22	16.5	9	12.3
Four	4	3.0	3	4.1
Five	2	1.5	—	—
Six	1	0.8	—	—
Total	133	100.0	73	100.0

Source: Compiled by the author.

The use of the marginal cost (or variable cost) method among the Japanese firms is rather limited. As shown in Table 5.13, none of the pricing companies used actual variable production cost as the transfer price. Seven U.S. firms and one Japanese firm reported that they used standard variable production cost as the transfer price. However, Table 5.14 indicates that only two U.S. companies and one Japanese firm used standard variable production cost as their dominant transfer prices.

None of the U.S. firms used mathematical programming to calculate the domestic transfer prices; only one Japanese company used it as a supplementary method. This Japanese firm manufactures paper products. Its programming method is shown below:

$$\text{Transfer price} = A + \frac{C}{D}$$

where A = standard variable cost of goods transferred
b = yield per day of goods transferred
c = main product's marginal profit per day

The above method is simpler than the decomposition procedure or the linear programming method mentioned in Chapter 2.

There seems to be a gap between the concepts advocated by many writers and those of practitioners with respect to the use of transfer prices. The concepts of marginal cost and opportunity cost, the decomposition procedure, and other programming methods have been advocated by many authorities in the past. However, the acceptance of these concepts or methods among large industrial firms in the United States and Japan appears to be minimal.

International Transfer Prices

Table 5.16 indicates the international transfer prices reported as being used by 85 U.S. and 42 Japanese companies to account for their international interdivisional transfers. Table 5.17 shows the dominant international transfer prices reported by these 127 companies.

As shown in Tables 5.16 and 5.17, full-production cost-plus was the most popular international transfer pricing method used among both U.S. and Japanese companies. Other widely used methods were market price, negotiated price, and market price less selling expenses. The wide application of the above four methods may have been due to the enforcement of Section 482 of the U.S. Internal Revenue Code and the sanctions of similar legislations in other countries.[3] Section 482 of the Internal Revenue Code reads as follows:

TABLE 5.16: Transfer Pricing Methods Used by the
Respondent Firms for International Transfers

| | United States | | Japan | |
Pricing Methods	Number of Firms	Percent of Total	Number of Firms	Percent of Total
Cost-oriented methods:				
Actual variable cost of production	0	0	1	1.6
Actual full-production cost	6	5.1	0	0
Standard variable cost of production	1	0.8	0	0
Standard full-production cost	6	5.1	3	4.8
Actual variable production cost plus a lump-sum subsidy	2	1.7	1	1.6
Full-production cost (actual or standard) plus some allowance for profit	38	32.2	21	33.3
Other cost-oriented methods	2	1.7	0	0
Subtotal for cost-oriented methods	55	46.6	26	41.3
Non-cost-oriented methods:				
Market price	24	20.4	14	22.2
Market price less selling expenses	17	14.4	9	14.3
Negotiated price	16	13.6	14	22.2
Mathematical programming price	1	0.8	0	0
Other non-cost-oriented methods	5	4.2	0	0
Subtotal for non-cost-oriented methods	63	53.4	37	58.7
Total—all methods	118	100.0	63	100.0

Source: Compiled by the author.

TABLE 5.17: The Dominant Transfer Pricing Methods
Used by the Respondent Firms for
International Transfers

Dominant Transfer Pricing Methods*	United States		Japan	
	Number of Firms	Percent of Total	Number of Firms	Percent of Total
Cost-oriented methods:				
Actual variable cost of production	0	0	1	2.4
Actual full-production cost	2	2.3	0	0
Standard variable cost of production	1	1.2	0	0
Standard full-production cost	3	3.5	2	4.7
Actual variable production cost plus a lump-sum subsidy	1	1.2	1	2.4
Full-production cost (actual or standard) plus some allowance for profit	31	36.5	15	35.7
Other cost-oriented methods	1	1.2	0	0
Subtotal for cost-oriented methods	39	45.9	19	45.2
Non-cost-oriented methods:				
Market price	18	21.2	11	26.2
Market price less selling expenses	9	10.6	5	11.9
Negotiated price	14	16.4	7	16.7
Mathematical programming price	1	1.2	0	0
Other non-cost-oriented methods	4	4.7	0	0
Subtotal for non-cost-oriented methods	46	54.1	23	54.8
Total—all methods	85	100.0	42	100.0

*Dominant international transfer price is the single or most important transfer pricing method used by the firm to account for international interdivisional transfers.

Source: Compiled by the author.

In any case of two or more organizations, trades, or businesses (whether or not incorporated, whether or not organized in the United States, and whether or not affiliated) owned or controlled directly or indirectly by the same interests, the Secretary or his delegate may distribute, apportion, or allocate gross income, deductions, credits, or allowances between or among such organizations, trades, or businesses, if he determines that such distribution, apportionment, or allocation is necessary in order to prevent evasion of taxes or clearly to reflect the income of any such organizations, trades, or businesses.

To implement Section 482, the Treasury Department adopted regulations applicable to all types of intercompany transactions. As described in Chapter 2, only three methods are specifically accepted for intercompany sales of tangible property in the regulation. But a fourth method provides for "some other appropriate method" that can be used only when none of the first three methods can reasonably be applied under the facts and circumstances as they exist in a particular case. Some practical means of setting, testing, and defending transfer prices under Section 482 regulations were suggested by Paul D. Seghers.[4] Michael G. Duerr reported that many U.S. MNCs have made minor or even major changes in their international operations as a result of Section 482.[5]

Table 5.18 indicates that 29.4 percent of U.S. respondents and 33.3 percent of Japanese respondents used more than one international transfer price. It can also be seen by comparing Table 5.18 with Table 5.15 that proportionately more respondent firms used one single transfer price to account for their international transfers than for domestic transfers.

By comparing Tables 5.16 and 5.17 with Tables 5.13 and 5.14, it may be seen that both the U.S. and Japanese international transfer prices were less cost-oriented than their domestic transfer prices. This was more evident in the U.S. firms than in the Japanese. As shown in Tables 5.14 and 5.17, although 56.4 percent of U.S. respondent firms used cost-oriented methods for their dominant domestic transfer prices, only 45.9 percent used cost-oriented methods for their dominant international transfer prices.

A comparison between Tables 5.14 and 5.17 also shows that there was a significantly greater use of full-production costs-plus as the dominant international transfer prices among both the U.S. and the Japanese firms. As shown in Table 5.14, only 24.1 percent of the U.S. firms used full-production costs-plus as their dominant domestic transfer pricing methods. However, Table 5.17 indicates

TABLE 5.18: The Number of International Transfer
Pricing Methods Used by the
Respondent Firms

Number of Methods Used	United States		Japan	
	Number of Companies	Percent of Total	Number of Companies	Percent of Total
One	60	70.6	28	66.7
Two	21	24.7	8	19.1
Three	2	2.4	5	11.9
Four			1	2.3
Five	2	2.3		
Total	85	100.0	42	100.0

Source: Compiled by the author.

that 36.5 percent of the U.S. firms used this method for their dominant international transfer prices. The similar shift is more dramatic
for the Japanese corporations. Only 15.1 percent of the Japanese
firms used full-production costs-plus as their dominant domestic
transfer prices, but 35.7 percent of the Japanese firms used this
method for their dominant international transfer prices.

As previously reported, the uses of mathematical programming
and the marginal cost concept were rather limited among the respondent firms in the two national groups. Only one U.S. firm used a
mathematical programming method to calculate its international
transfer prices, and this company is in the office equipment industry.
It described its programming price as "price calculated to share
profit or loss on the transaction in proportion to parent/subsidiary
respective fully loaded costs."

It may be seen from Table 5.17 that one Japanese company and
one U.S. firm used actual variable costs-plus as their dominant
international transfer prices. These two firms may have sold their
merchandise in foreign markets at prices lower than in the home
market (country of origin). Although there is no evidence that they
were doing so, there is a possibility that a firm using variable cost
as the international transfer price may be practicing "dumping"
according to the U.S. Antidumping Act.[6] However, this study did
not indicate any sign of widespread practices of dumping in foreign
markets among either large U.S. or Japanese industrial companies.

TESTING OF HYPOTHESES RELATED TO
TRANSFER PRICING METHODS

The results of the tests of six hypotheses related to transfer pricing methods (A-1, A-2, B-1, B-2, B-3, and B-4) are reported in this section. Those readers who are more interested in the practical rather than the theoretical aspects of transfer pricing may omit this section and proceed directly to the "Summary" section at the end of this chapter.

In testing the hypotheses on transfer pricing methods, a chi-square test was used because the data could be classified into contingency tables.[7] Hypothesis A-1 states that the extent of application of cost-oriented or non-cost-oriented domestic transfer prices among large American (that is, U.S.) industrial companies (LAIC) and large Japanese industrial companies (LJIC) does not vary according to the nationality of these firms. This hypothesis was tested using the relationship between nationality and the use of cost-oriented or non-cost-oriented domestic transfer prices among respondent firms as shown in Table 5.19. The hypothesis was also tested using the relationship between nationality and the use of cost-oriented or non-cost-oriented dominant domestic transfer prices as shown in Table 5.20. Neither of the two tests shows that the computed chi-square

TABLE 5.19: Nationality and the Use of Cost-Oriented
or Non-Cost-Oriented Domestic Transfer
Prices Among the Respondent Firms

Domestic Transfer Pricing Methods	United States	Japan	Total
Cost-oriented	117	55	172
Non-cost-oriented	115	64	179
Total	232	119	351

Computed chi-square value = .403
Chi-square (Table value):
  at 5 percent significance level = 3.841
  at 10 percent significance level = 2.706
Conclusion: The relationship is not significant

Source: Compiled by the author.

TABLE 5.20: Nationality and the Use of Cost-Oriented or Non-Cost-Oriented Dominant Domestic Transfer Prices Among the Respondent Firms

Dominant Domestic Transfer Pricing Method*	United States	Japan	Total
Cost-oriented	75	34	109
Non-cost-oriented	58	39	97
Total	133	73	206

Computed chi-square value = 1.450
Chi-square (Table value):
at 5 percent significance level = 3.841
at 10 percent significance level = 2.706
Conclusion: The relationship is not significant

*The dominant domestic transfer pricing method is the single or most important transfer price used by a firm to account for domestic interdivisional transfers.

Source: Compiled by the author.

value was large enough to reject hypothesis A-1 at a significance level of 10 percent. Therefore, it was concluded that the orientation of the domestic transfer prices of Japanese firms is not significantly different from that of the U.S. firms.

Hypothesis A-2 states that the extent of application of cost-oriented or non-cost-oriented international transfer prices among LAIC and LJIC does not vary according to the nationality of these companies. The hypothesis was first tested using the relationship between nationality and the use of cost-oriented or non-cost-oriented international transfer prices among sample firms as shown in Table 5.21. It was tested again using the relationship between nationality and the use of cost-oriented or non-cost-oriented dominant international transfer prices as indicated in Table 5.22. Both tests show that the computed chi-square values were not large enough to reject hypothesis A-1 at a 10 percent significance level. Therefore, it was concluded that the orientation of the international transfer prices of Japanese firms is not significantly different from that of the U.S. firms.

TABLE 5.21: Nationality and the Use of Cost-Oriented
or Non-Cost-Oriented International Transfer
Prices Among the Respondent Firms

International Transfer Pricing Methods	United States	Japan	Total
Cost-oriented	55	26	81
Non-cost-oriented	63	37	100
Total	118	63	181

Computed chi-square value = .282
Chi-square (Table value):
at 5 percent significance level = 3.841
at 10 percent significance level = 2.706
Conclusion: The relationship is not significant

Source: Compiled by the author.

TABLE 5.22: Nationality and the Use of Cost-Oriented or
Non-Cost-Oriented Dominant International
Transfer Prices Among the Respondent Firms

Dominant International Transfer Pricing Methods*	United States	Japan	Total
Cost-oriented	39	19	58
Non-cost-oriented	46	23	69
Total	85	42	127

Computed chi-square value = .015
Chi-square (Table value):
at 5 percent significance level = 3.841
at 10 percent significance level = 2.706
Conclusion: The relationship is not significant

*The dominant international transfer pricing method is the
single or most important transfer price used by a firm for international interdivisional transfers.

Source: Compiled by the author.

The test results of hypothesis A-2 do not support Arpan's conclusion that "U.S. systems of international intracorporate pricing are distinctly more cost-oriented . . . than non-U.S. systems."[8] The results of the tests of hypotheses A-1 and A-2 also do not support Arpan's observation that the Japanese prefer cost-oriented systems.[9]

Total revenue was used as the measure of size in the testing of hypotheses B-1, B-2, B-3, and B-4. The use of cost-oriented or non-cost-oriented methods for the dominant domestic transfer prices or international transfer prices was classified into contingency tables and chi-square values were computed. These chi-square values were then compared with the significant values obtained from the chi-square distribution table to see if there were significant relationships between the size factor and use of the cost-oriented or the non-cost-oriented method.

Hypothesis B-1 states that the extent of usage of cost-oriented transfer prices for domestic interdivisional transfers among LAIC is not related to the size of these companies. Table 5.23 shows that the calculated chi-square value was 4.068. This was not significant at either a 5 percent or a 10 percent significance level; therefore,

TABLE 5.23: Total Revenues and the Orientation of
Dominant Domestic Transfer Prices
of the U.S. Firms

Dominant Transfer Pricing Method	Size Classification (in U.S. $ million)					Total
	Less than 100	100–200	200–400	400–1,000	Above 1,000	
Cost-oriented	2	18	20	22	13	75
Non-cost-oriented	3	14	12	12	17	58
Total	5	32	32	34	30	133

Computed chi-square value = 4.068
Chi-square (Table value):
 at 5 percent significance level = 9.488
 at 10 percent significance level = 7.779
Conclusion: The relationship is not significant

Source: Compiled by the author.

TABLE 5.24: Total Revenues and the Orientation of
Dominant Domestic Transfer Prices
of the Japanese Firms

Dominant Transfer Pricing Method	Size Classification (in U.S. $ million)					Total
	Less than 100	100–200	200–400	400–1,000	Above 1,000	
Cost-oriented	5	9	9	10	1	34
Non-cost-oriented	1	3	15	11	9	39
Total	6	12	24	21	10	73

Computed chi-square value = 13.334
Chi-square (Table value):
    at 1 percent significance level = 13.277
    at 5 percent significance level = 9.488
    at 10 percent significance level = 7.779
Conclusion: The relationship is significant at 1 percent
    level

Source: Compiled by the author.

there is no significant relationship between the size of U.S. companies and the orientation of the domestic transfer prices used by these companies.

Hypothesis B-2 states that the extent of usage of cost-oriented transfer prices for domestic interdivisional transfers among LJIC is not related to the size of these companies. In Table 5.24, a chi-square value of 13.334 was computed. This was significant at 1 percent significance level. Hence, there is a significant relationship between the size of Japanese firms and the use of cost-oriented or non-cost-oriented transfer price. After examining the data in Table 5.24, it was found that the larger the size of the Japanese company, the more likely will be the use of a non-cost-oriented domestic transfer price.

Hypothesis B-3 states that the extent of usage of cost-oriented transfer prices for international interdivisional transfers among LAIC is not related to the size of these companies. In Table 5.25, a chi-square value of 2.552 was obtained. Since the value is less

than 7.779, it is not high enough to reject the null hypothesis at a
10 percent significance level. Therefore, the relationship between
the size of U.S. firms and the use of cost-oriented or non-cost-
oriented international transfer price was not significant.

Hypothesis B-4 states that the extent of usage of cost-oriented
transfer prices for <u>international</u> interdivisional transfers among
LJIC is not related to the size of these companies. In Table 5.26,
a chi-square value of 13.827 was computed. Since this value is
higher than 13.277, a value needed to reject to a null hypothesis at
a 1 percent significance level, hypothesis B-4 is rejected. It was
concluded that a significant relationship exists between the size of
Japanese firms and the use of cost-oriented or non-cost-oriented
international transfer pricing methods. An examination of Table
5.26 indicates that the larger the size of the Japanese firms, the
more likely is the use of non-cost-oriented international transfer
prices.

The results of the statistical tests of hypotheses B-1, B-2,
B-3, and B-4 described above do not support Arpan's conclusion
that "the larger the parent firm, the more likely it is to use a cost-

TABLE 5.25: Total Revenues and the Orientation of
Dominant International Transfer Prices
of the U.S. Firms

Dominant Transfer Pricing Method	Size Classification (in U.S. $ million)					
	Less than 100	100– 200	200– 400	400– 1,000	Above 1,000	Total
Cost-oriented	1	11	9	8	10	39
Non-cost-oriented	0	9	10	11	16	46
Total	1	20	19	19	26	85

Computed chi-square value = 2.552
Chi-square (Table value):
at 5 percent significance level = 9.488
at 10 percent significance level = 7.779
Conclusion: The relationship is not significant

Source: Compiled by the author.

TABLE 5.26: Total Revenues and the Orientation of
Dominant International Transfer Prices
of the Japanese Firms

Dominant Transfer Pricing Method	Less than 100	100–200	200–400	400–1,000	Above 1,000	Total
Cost-oriented	3	6	8	1	1	19
Non-cost-oriented	0	2	7	6	8	23
Total	3	8	15	7	9	42

Computed chi-square value = 13.827
Chi-square (Table value):
   at 1 percent significance level = 13.277
   at 5 percent significance level = 9.488
   at 10 percent significance level = 7.779
Conclusion: The relationship is significant at 1 percent
      level

Source: Compiled by the author.

oriented system."[10] In fact, among the Japanese companies, it was
shown that the opposite is true, that is, the larger the size of the
Japanese industrial companies, the more likely was the use of non-
cost-oriented transfer prices for either domestic or international
interdivisional transfers.

SUMMARY

The characteristics of respondent firms and their transfer
pricing methods were described in this chapter. The respondent
firms included 145 U.S. and 102 Japanese large industrial corporations and they represent a wide variety of industries from the two
countries. It was found that respondents in both national groups were
comparable in terms of total revenue, exports to and imports from
foreign subsidiaries, and percentage of interdivisional transfers to
total revenue. Nevertheless, the scale of operations of U.S. MNCs
was broader than that of the Japanese MNCs.

In percentage terms, more U.S. firms used transfer prices than Japanese companies. The main reason cited by a majority of nonusers of transfer prices was that their interdivisional transfers were insignificant. The total number of domestic transfer pricing methods used by either U.S. or Japanese companies was about equally divided between the cost-oriented and non-cost-oriented methods. The international transfer prices used by both the U.S. and Japanese companies were less cost-oriented than their domestic transfer prices.

Statistical tests of hypotheses show that there were no significant difference between the orientations of transfer prices used by the Japanese and the U.S. firms. Also, it was found that the extent of usage of cost-oriented transfer prices among the U.S. firms is not related to the size of these companies. In contrast, the larger the size of the Japanese company, the more likely will be the use of a non-cost-oriented transfer price, for either domestic or international interdivisional transfers.

NOTES

1. Business International, October 14, 1977, pp. 324-25.
2. See Willard E. Stone, "Management Practices with Respect to Internal Transfer Pricing in Large Manufacturing Companies," (Ph.D. dissertation, University of Pennsylvania, 1957), p. 54. Stone's sample was selected from a list of 1,000 large U.S. manufacturing companies compiled by the U.S. Federal Trade Commission in 1951.
3. See Business International Corporation, Setting Intercorporate Pricing Policies (New York, 1973), p. 41. The countries that have legislation resembling Section 482 of the U.S. Internal Revenue Code are Belgium, Canada, France, Italy, Sweden, Switzerland, and the United Kingdom. German Federal Republic, Japan, and the Netherlands did not have specific provisions similar to Section 482, but the governments of these countries may insist upon a fair allocation of profit between related companies.
4. Paul D. Seghers, "How to Set and Defend Intercompany Prices under Section 482 Regulations," Taxes 47 (October 1969): 606-22.
5. Michael G. Duerr, Tax Allocations and International Business (New York: The Conference Board, 1972), pp. 56-63.
6. See Section 201 of the Antidumping Act, 1921.
7. W. J. Conoven, Practical Nonparametric Statistics (New York: John Wiley and Sons, 1971), pp. 140-201.
8. Jeffrey S. Arpan, International Intracorporate Pricing: Non-American Systems and Views (New York: Praeger, 1972), p. 109.

9. Ibid., p. 84.
10. Ibid., p. 79.

6

FINDINGS AND ANALYSIS: ENVIRONMENTAL VARIABLES AND OTHER ISSUES

This chapter continues the presentation of the major findings and results of the research. First of all, the responses of the U.S. and Japanese corporations on environmental variables of international transfer pricing will be discussed. Then, the objectives and major policies related to these corporations' transfer pricing systems will be analyzed. Results from the interviews with two partners in international accounting firms will also be presented. Finally, the results of a nonresponse bias test will be reported.

ENVIRONMENTAL VARIABLES

When a company formulates its international transfer pricing policies, it normally has to consider a host of variables in the international environment as well as internal factors within the firm. The external environmental variables include income tax legislation, customs duties, competition, and inflation. The internal factors of the company may include profits, divisional performance evaluation, volume of interdivisional transfers, and so forth. Analysis of environmental variables and their potential impacts on international transfer pricing can be found in the studies by Arpan, Greene and Duerr, and Shulman.[1] Some of the more important findings of these studies are presented in Chapter 2.

The main purposes of this section are to determine the more important environmental variables considered by large U.S. and Japanese MNCs in formulating their international transfer pricing policies and to explain the differences between the two national groups in the consideration of environmental variables. One difficult task during the early stage of the study was to develop a representative list of variables usually considered by MNCs. After reviewing the literature, a list of 15 environmental variables was developed, and these were tested in the pilot study. This preliminary list and the results of the pilot study were discussed with business educators and experienced public accountants in the United States and Canada. After careful consideration of their suggestions, the list was expanded from 15 to 20 variables as shown in Table 6.1; these variables were used in the revised questionnaire for the full-scale study.

An Overview of the Results

In the full-scale study, 88 U.S. and 57 Japanese companies answered all or part of the questions on environmental variables. Respondents were asked to rate the importance of each variable on a five-point scale as follows:

Extremely Important	Very Important	Moderately Important	Not too Important	Not at all Important
5	4	3	2	1

The mean rating of a particular variable was computed by adding the integer values assigned to the variable and then dividing the sum by the number of firms. Table 6.1 shows the mean ratings and the ranking of mean ratings by national group. To facilitate comparison, the ordering of the variables follows the rankings by the U.S. firms.

One significant result from the analysis was that Japanese mean ratings on all 20 variables were consistently higher than those of the U.S. firms. A possible interpretation of this phenomenon is that different measurement scales might have been used by the two national groups in responding to the questionnaire. However, an extensive search of the literature by the author failed to find any study dealing with the differences in the behavioral patterns of U.S. and Japanese industrial firms in performing a task similar to the one in this study. Another possible interpretation is that foreign trade is more important to the Japanese than to the U.S. economy. As shown in Tables 6.2 and 6.3, the average percentage of Japan's foreign trade to their gross national products (GNPs) from 1973 to 1977 was 22.7 percent, whereas the U.S. foreign trade accounted for only an average of 13.7 percent of their GNP for the same five-year period.

It can be seen from Table 6.1 that overall profit received the highest rating by both groups. It is not surprising to see that profit is the most important consideration among the respondent firms in formulating their international transfer pricing policies.

TABLE 6.1: Rank Order and Mean Rating of Importance of Environmental Variables

Ranking of Mean Rating		Variables	Mean Rating	
United States	Japan		United States	Japan
1	1	Overall profit to the company	3.9432	3.9474
2	4	Restrictions imposed by foreign countries on repatriation of profits or dividends	3.2353	3.5962
3	2	The competitive position of subsidiaries in foreign countries	3.1628	3.9123
4	14	Differentials in income tax rates and income tax legislation among countries	3.0581	3.2075
5	5	Performance evaluation of foreign subsidiaries	3.0115	3.4717
6	9	Rate of customs duties and customs legislation where the company has operations	2.9885	3.3962
7	11	Import restrictions imposed by foreign countries	2.8851	3.3462
8	12	Restrictions imposed by foreign countries on the amount of royalty or management fees that can be charged against foreign subsidiaries	2.8488	3.3269

9	6,7	The need to maintain adequate cash flows in foreign subsidiaries	2.8256	3.4528
10	15	Rules and requirements of financial reporting for foreign subsidiaries	2.7791	3.0962
11	10	Maintaining good relationships with host governments	2.7529	3.3654
12	3	Devaluation and revaluation in countries where the company has operations	2.7126	3.7255
13	8	Rates of inflation in foreign countries	2.5747	3.4038
14	18	Volume of interdivisional transfers	2.5294	2.9423
15	13	Antidumping legislation of foreign countries	2.4483	3.2885
16	16	The need of subsidiaries in foreign countries to seek local funds	2.4000	3.0577
17	6,7	The interests of local partners of foreign subsidiaries	2.2963	3.4528
18	20	Domestic government requirements on direct foreign investments	2.2651	2.6538
19	17	Risk of expropriation in foreign countries where the company has operations	2.2262	3.0385
20	19	Antitrust legislation of foreign countries	2.1412	2.7692

Source: Compiled by the author.

81

Four other variables to which high ratings were given by the U.S. firms are restrictions on repatriation of profits or dividends, competitive position of foreign subsidiaries, income tax, and performance evaluation. The Japanese also gave high ratings to competitive position of foreign subsidiaries, restrictions on repatriation of profits and dividends, and performance evaluation; however, income tax was ranked lower among the Japanese firms. Contrary to the ratings of U.S. firms, devaluation and revaluation was given higher ratings by the Japanese firms.

Surprisingly, some variables—including antitrust legislation, risk of expropriation, and domestic government requirements on direct, foreign investments—were given relatively low ratings by both national groups, suggesting that these variables are less important to the Japanese and U.S. firms in the formulation of international transfer pricing policies.

In order to find out whether the ranking of mean ratings by the two national groups on all 20 variables was correlated, two rank order tests—the Kendall correlation coefficient and the Spearman correlation coefficient[2]—were conducted. The tests were based on the rank data in Table 6.1. The computed Kendall rank correlation

TABLE 6.2: Japan's Foreign Trade as a Percentage of
Gross National Products, 1973-77
(money amounts in billions of yens)

Year	Exports	Imports (c.i.f.)	Total Foreign Trade	GNP*	Foreign Trade as a Percentage of GNP
1973	10,031	10,404	20,435	111,091	18.4
1974	16,208	18,076	34,284	132,362	25.9
1975	16,572	17,174	33,746	145,654	23.2
1976	19,930	19,229	39,159	164,420	23.8
1977	21,660	19,128	40,788	183,600	22.2
		Five-year average (1973-77)			22.7

*At current price.

Source: International Monetary Fund, International Financial Statistics (Washington, D.C.: IMF, various issues).

TABLE 6.3: U.S. Foreign Trade as a Percentage of
Gross National Products, 1973-77

Year	Exports (millions U.S. $)	Imports (millions U.S. $)	Total Foreign Trade (millions U.S. $)	GNP* (billions U.S. $)	Foreign Trade as a Percentage of GNP
1973	71,339	73,575	114,914	1,306.6	11.1
1974	98,507	107,996	206,503	1,412.9	14.6
1975	107,592	103,389	210,981	1,528.8	13.8
1976	114,992	129,565	244,557	1,706.5	14.3
1977	120,164	156,695	276,859	1,889.6	14.7
		Five-year average (1973-77)			13.7

*At current price.

Source: International Monetary Fund, International Financial Statistics (Washington, D.C.: IMF, various issues).

coefficient was .544 and the Spearman correlation coefficient was .695. In both tests, the significance levels were set at .001. The results show that there was a moderate correlation between the ranking of variables by the two groups. In other words, both subject groups had some agreement on the relative importance of the 20 variables. A t test of all the significant differences between the ratings (absolute importance) by the two groups on all 20 variables will be discussed later, when a hypothesis related to environmental variables is tested.

A Discussion of the More Important
Environmental Variables

The respondent firms were concerned about restrictions on repatriation of profits or dividends because many countries have such restrictions. For example, in Argentina, "in times of exchange restrictions and balance of payment difficulties, the right to repatriate capital and remit profits may be suspended."[3] In Italy, the remittance of dividends and profits per year is limited to a maximum of 8 percent of capital investment.[4] One way to cope with these

restrictions is to increase the prices for interdivisional transfers
to subsidiaries in those countries.

Transfer prices may be used to strengthen the competitive
position of foreign subsidiaries and to weaken the position of com-
petitors, or to mitigate the internal effects of outside competition.
This can be done by reducing the transfer prices to these foreign
subsidiaries.[5] In addition other methods may be used to improve
foreign subsidiaries' positions. Several Japanese companies have
successfully improved the competitive positions of their U.S. subsidiaries by adopting a management style that emphasizes quality
control, encourages strong worker loyalty, and requires an inordinate
devotion to details.[6]

Income tax consideration was given high ratings among many
MNCs, notably several large U.S. companies. This is because
corporate profits may be affected by differentials in income tax rates
and income tax legislation among countries. Table 6.4 shows the
corporate income tax rates and dividend withholding tax rates of
36 selected countries. One can see significant differences among
the tax rates of several countries. Most MNCs can take advantage
of these differences as suggested by Shulman:

> Greater profits will result from shipping goods into
> low income tax countries at prices which are lowered
> in order to raise income in such countries. And if
> prices of goods shipped from such countries to the
> United States are set high, the rate differential may
> result in maximizing corporate profits in both coun-
> tries.[7]

However, more and more countries are becoming aware of this kind
of tactic practiced by many MNCs, and these countries are taking
actions to scrutinize the transfer pricing practices of MNCs.[8]
Experts of the United Nations Commission on Transnational Corporations (UNCTC) are also in the process of developing new accounting
standards that may eventually force MNCs to disclose the important
aspects of their transfer pricing policies.[9]

Performance evaluation was also given high rating by both
national groups. This is consistent with another finding from the
research, that is, determining subsidiaries' performances was one
of the two major objectives of the transfer pricing systems of respondent firms. The other major objective was to maximize consolidated
profit of the company. Findings related to objectives of transfer
pricing systems will be discussed later in this chapter.

Several writers have emphasized the importance of performance
evaluation. Shulman considered evaluation to be one of the three

basic requirements vital to the promotion of corporate effectiveness.[10] The other requirements are measurement and motivation. Shilling-law also considered evaluation important and warned against the manipulation of transfer price to influence performance evaluation. He stated:

> The danger is that top management will allow the trans-
> fer price to influence its appraisal of the division
> managers' performance, or, which amounts to the
> same thing, that the division managers will think the
> transfer price is affecting their performance ratings
> unfairly. This can lead to dissension and can even
> defeat the main purpose of profit decentralization by
> impairing the managers' motivations to produce
> profits.[11]

Major Differences between the
Two National Groups

Noticeable differences between the ratings of the two national groups can be found in two variables: devaluation and revaluation of foreign currencies and the interests of local partners in foreign subsidiaries. Compared to U.S. firms, the Japanese companies placed significantly greater importance on these variables, as can be seen in Table 6.1.

The Japanese have good reasons to worry about devaluation and revaluation because the U.S. dollar, the currency of the most important trading partner of Japan, has fallen sharply in recent years. As mentioned in Chapter 3, the monthly average exchange rate in units of yen per U.S. dollar declined by 26 percent between January 1977 and June 1978. The adverse effect of the revaluation of yen to the Japanese business community is described in Chapter 3. Further appreciation of the yen is considered likely.

Japanese companies have to place greater emphasis on the interests of local partners because many foreign subsidiaries of the Japanese firms are located in South Korea, Taiwan, and other developing countries. In fact, over 50 percent of Japanese overseas investment is in the developing regions including the Far East, the Middle East, and Africa.[12] In contrast, over 60 percent of U.S. direct foreign investment is in the developed countries such as Canada, Western Europe, and Australia.[13] Governments of many developing countries require local ownership of major portions of the subsidiaries of foreign companies.

TABLE 6.4: Corporate Income Tax Rates and Dividend-Withholding Tax Rates of Selected Countries (percent)

Country	Corporate Income Tax Rate[a]	Dividend Withholding Tax Rate[b]
North America		
United States	48.0	30.0
Canada	46.0	25.0
Europe		
Belgium:		
Domestic corp.	48.0	20.0
Branch of foreign co.	54.0	
Denmark	37.0	30.0
France	50.0	25.0
Federal Republic of Germany		
Domestic corp.		
Undistributed	56.0	25.0
Distributed	36.0	
Branch of foreign co.	50.0	
Ireland	45.0	35.0
Italy	25.0	30.0

Country	Corporate Income Tax Rate[a]	Dividend Withholding Tax Rate[b]
Latin America		
Argentina:		
Domestic corp.	33.0	17.5
Branch of foreign co.	45.0	
Brazil	30.0	25.0
Chile	15.0	40.0
Columbia	40.0	20.0
Mexico	42.0	21.0
Panama	50.0	10.0
Peru	55.0	30.0
Venezuela	50.0	15.0
East Asia		
India		
Domestic corp.	55.0	25.0
Branch of foreign co.	70.0	
Indonesia	45.0	20.0

Luxembourg	40.0	15.0
Netherlands	48.0	25.0
United Kingdom	52.0	0
Norway:		
Undistributed	50.8	25.0
Distributed	23.0	
Spain	36.0	16.5
Sweden	40.0	30.0
Switzerland	3.63–40.0	35.0
Australasia		
Australia	46.0	30.0
New Zealand		
Domestic corp.	45.0	15.0
Branch of foreign co.	50.0	
Africa		
Liberia	50.0	15.0
Libya	60.0	0
South Africa	43.0	15.0
Japan:		
Domestic corp.		
Undistributed	40.0	20.0
Distributed	30.0	
Branch of foreign co.	40.0	
Philippines	35.0	35.0
Middle East		
Iran:		
Domestic corp.	13.4	60.0
Branch of foreign co.	60.0	
Kuwait:		
Domestic corp.	0	0
Branch of foreign co.	55.0	
Lebanon	44.0	0
Saudi Arabia	45.0	0

aFor countries with graduated income tax structures, rates listed are the maximum rates that can be applied.

bDividend withholding rates listed do not take into account tax treaty reductions.

Note: All corporate income and dividend withholding tax rates listed were in effect as of December 31, 1977.

Source: Compiled by the author.

The presence of local partners limits the flexibility of the parent company in determining transfer prices because the local partners are anxious to obtain the lowest possible transfer price (for intermediate goods transferred from the parent company) to assure that maximum profit is accrued to the subsidiary. In a study on the pattern of organizational evolution of 50 major Japanese manufacturing companies, M. Y. Yoshino found that transfer price was a frequent source of conflict between Japanese parent companies and their joint venture partners in foreign subsidiaries, especially during the early stages of these joint ventures.[14] During the early stages, the joint ventures are heavily dependent on the Japanese parent companies for supplies of materials and components.

Testing of Hypothesis

The hypothesis tested here is C-1, which states that there is no significant difference between the absolute importance placed upon each of the major environmental variables by LAIC and LJIC when they formulate their international transfer pricing policies. A simple t test at the 1 percent level ($\alpha = .01$) was used to detect any significant differences.[15] The t values and their two-tailed probabilities for all 20 variables are shown in Table 6.5.

The results show that hypothesis C-1 was rejected for 10 of the 20 variables. Those variables for which hypothesis C-1 was rejected are labeled "S" (or "significant"). This means that the differences between the absolute importance placed upon these variables by the two national groups were significant. The other 10 variables on which the hypothesis was not rejected are labeled "NS" (or "not significant"), which means that the differences between the absolute importance placed upon these variables by U.S. and Japanese companies were not significant. The test result described above provides little support to one of Arpan's conclusions, that is, that the very large MNCs of all nationalities exhibit the smallest differences in views of attendant problems.[16]

OTHER POLICIES AND ISSUES ON
TRANSFER PRICING

The revised questionnaire contained several questions on other major policies and issues related to transfer pricing. This was designed to find the key objectives of the transfer pricing systems of the respondent firms, the authority of determining transfer pricing policies, means by which policy disagreements were settled, and

TABLE 6.5: t Statistic and Two-Tail Probability of Each Environmental Variable

Variables (Order on Questionnaire)	Degree of Freedom	t Statistic	Two-Tail Probability	Test* Results
Overall profit to the company (11)	143	-0.02	.982	NS
Restrictions imposed by foreign countries on repatriation of profits or dividends (12)	135	-1.78	.078	NS
The competitive position of subsidiaries in foreign countries (10)	141	-3.46	.001	S
Differentials in income tax rates and income tax legislation among countries (1)	137	-0.68	.496	NS
Performance evaluation of foreign subsidiaries (15)	138	-2.34	.021	NS
Rate of customs duties and customs legislation where the company has operations (2)	138	-1.87	.063	NS
Import restrictions imposed by foreign countries (13)	137	-2.16	.032	NS
Restrictions imposed by foreign countries on the amount of royalty or management fees that can be charged against foreign subsidiaries (19)	136	-2.22	.028	NS
The need to maintain adequate cash flows in foreign subsidiaries (20)	137	-2.89	.004	S
Rules and requirements of financial reporting for foreign subsidiaries (16)	136	-1.66	.100	NS

(continued)

Table 6.5 (continued)

Variables (Order on Questionnaire)	Degree of Freedom	t Statistic	Two–Tail Probability	Test* Results
Maintaining good relationships with host governments (9)	135	-2.92	.004	S
Devaluation and revaluation in countries where the company has operations (8)	136	-4.89	.000	S
Rates of inflation in foreign countries (5)	137	-4.22	.000	S
Volume of interdivisional transfers (17)	135	-2.18	.031	NS
Antidumping legislation of foreign countries (4)	137	-3.64	.000	S
The need of subsidiaries in foreign countries to seek local funds (14)	135	-3.44	.000	S
The interests of local partners of foreign subsidiaries (7)	132	-5.43	.000	S
Domestic government requirements on direct foreign investments (18)	133	-2.04	.043	NS
Risk of expropriation in foreign countries where the company has operations (6)	134	-3.67	.000	S
Antitrust legislation of foreign countries (3)	135	-3.24	.001	S

*S = significant; NS = not significant.
Source: Compiled by the author.

the respondent firms' policies on outside purchases of raw materials and intermediate products. The results are discussed as follows.

Key Objectives

In the questionnaire, each respondent was asked to point out the single or dominant corporate objective of the transfer pricing system. The responses are shown in Table 6.6. Percentage-wise, the distributions of the various objectives between the two national groups appear to be quite similar. Maximizing consolidated profit and determining divisional performances were the two most important objectives mentioned by both Japanese and U.S. respondent com-

TABLE 6.6: A Comparison of the Dominant Transfer Pricing Objectives of U.S. and Japanese Respondent Firms

	United States		Japan	
	No. of Firms	Percent of Total	No. of Firms	Percent of Total
Maximize consolidated profits of the company	57	41.0	33	41.8
Minimize payments on income taxes, customs duties, and other taxes paid to domestic government and foreign countries	10	7.2	4	5.0
Maximize sales volume	7	5.0	9	11.4
Determine the performances of domestic and foreign subsidiaries	58	41.8	30	38.0
Others	7	5.0	3	3.8
Total	139[a]	100.0	79[b]	100.0

[a]Six U.S. companies that used transfer prices named two dominant objectives.

[b]Four Japanese corporations that had transfer prices provided two dominant objectives.

Source: Compiled by the author.

panies. About 11 percent of the Japanese firms replied that they considered maximizing sales volume their key objective whereas only 5 percent of U.S. firms did so. Minimizing taxes and customs duties payments were reported by 7.2 percent of the U.S. firms and 5 percent of the Japanese firms as their key objectives.

The Authority of Determining Transfer
Pricing Policies

Table 6.7 compares the authority of determining transfer pricing policies among the U.S. and Japanese respondent firms. It may be inferred that the policy formulation process was primarily a centralized function handled by parent company executives. This is true for the majority of both the U.S. and the Japanese respondents. Similar findings were obtained by Arpan[17] and Larson[18] in their studies.

TABLE 6.7: A Comparison of the Authority for
Determining Transfer Pricing Policies
of the Respondent Firms

	United States		Japan	
	No. of Firms	Percent of Total	No. of Firms	Percent of Total
Top executives of parent company without prior consultation with divisional executives	45	34.1	11	14.9
Divisional executives themselves	32	24.2	26	35.1
Top executives of parent company after close consultation with divisional executives	54	40.9	37	50.0
Other method	1	0.8	—	—
Total	132*	100.0	74	100.0

*One U.S. company that used transfer prices did not answer this question.
Source: Compiled by the author.

As shown in Table 6.7, the transfer pricing policies of 34.1 percent of the U.S. firms were determined by the top executives from the parent companies without any prior consultation with divisional executives, whereas 40.9 percent of the firms had close consultation with their divisional management. About 24 percent of the U.S. firms permitted their divisional executives to determine their own policies.

Relatively speaking, Japanese firms were more decentralized than U.S. firms in the determination of transfer pricing policies. Although the policies of 14.9 percent of the Japanese firms were determined exclusively by the parent companies, 50 percent of the firms had close consultation with divisional management and 35.1 percent allowed the divisional management to establish their own policies.

The above findings also indicate that decision making by "consensus" is still widely used among Japanese firms as a tool to formulate transfer pricing practices. Under this approach, a proposed decision will be debated throughout the organization until there is agreement on it. Only then do the Japanese make the decision.[19]

How Policy Disagreements Were Settled

In the questionnaire, the U.S. and Japanese corporations were asked whether there have been any policy disagreements among their divisions on transfer pricing during the past two years. There were 133 U.S. and 74 Japanese companies that responded to this question. Of the 133 U.S. firms, 65 (49 percent) reported that they had policy disagreements. Only 24 Japanese companies (32 percent) indicated that they had policy disagreements during the past two years.

Table 6.8 shows how these 65 U.S. firms and 24 Japanese companies resolved their policy disagreements among divisions. Of U.S. firms, 36 (55 percent) settled their disagreements through financial executives from the parent companies whereas only 8.3 percent of the Japanese companies did the same. A substantial number of Japanese firms (87.5 percent) settled their disagreements through negotiation between the divisions involved, whereas only 32.3 percent of the U.S. corporations did so. A few companies had committees set up earlier to resolve their disagreements.

Policies on Outside Purchases of Raw
Materials and Intermediate Products

Tables 6.9 and 6.10 show the outside purchasing policies of U.S. and Japanese firms for their domestic divisions and foreign

TABLE 6.8: A Comparison of the Ways Policy
Disagreements Were Settled among
U.S. and Japanese Respondent Firms

	United States		Japan	
	No. of Firms	Percent of Total	No. of Firms	Percent of Total
Financial executives from the parent company	36	55.4	2	8.3
Negotiation between the divisions involved	21	32.3	21	87.5
Through a committee established earlier to settle the disagreement	3	4.6	1	4.2
Other methods	5	7.7	0	0
Number of companies that had policy disagreements among divisions	65	100.0	24	100.0

Source: Compiled by the author.

subsidiaries. It may be seen from Table 6.9 that 40 U.S. firms
(31.5 percent) allowed their domestic divisions to freely purchase
their raw materials and intermediate products from outside sources
whereas only 11 Japanese companies (15.3 percent) did so. About
55 percent of the U.S. and 40 percent of the Japanese companies
allowed outside purchases after the parent companies approved the
purchases. Thirty-two Japanese firms (44.4 percent) did not allow
their domestic divisions to purchase intermediate products or raw
materials from outside sources but only 17 U.S. firms (13.4 percent)
adhered to that policy. It appears, therefore, that the outside purchasing policies of Japanese firms for their domestic divisions were
more restrictive than those of the U.S. firms.

As shown in Table 6.10, the outside purchasing policies of
Japanese firms for their foreign divisions were also more restrictive
than those of the U.S. firms. However, a comparison between
Tables 6.9 and 6.10 shows that the outside purchasing policies of
Japanese firms with respect to foreign divisions were less restrictive
than those for domestic divisions.

TABLE 6.9: A Comparison of Outside Purchasing
Policies for Domestic Divisions of U.S.
and Japanese Respondent Firms

	United States		Japan	
	No. of Firms	Percent of Total	No. of Firms	Percent of Total
Allow outside purchases with complete freedom	40	31.5	11	15.3
Allow outside purchases subject to the approval of parent company	70	55.1	29	40.3
Outside purchases not allowed	17	13.4	32	44.4
Total	127[a]	100.0	72[b]	100.0

[a]Six U.S. companies that had domestic transfer prices did not answer this part of the questionnaire.

[b]One Japanese company that had domestic transfer prices did not answer this part of the questionnaire.

Source: Compiled by the author.

TABLE 6.10: A Comparison of Outside Purchasing
Policies for Foreign Divisions of U.S.
and Japanese Respondent Companies

	United States		Japan	
	No. of Firms	Percent of Total	No. of Firms	Percent of Total
Allow outside purchases with complete freedom	32	37.6	9	21.9
Allow outside purchases subject to the approval of parent company	39	45.9	20	48.8
Outside purchases not allowed	14	16.5	12	29.3
Total	85	100.0	41[*]	100.0

[*]One Japanese company that had international transfer price did not respond to this question.

Source: Compiled by the author.

INTERVIEWS WITH PARTNERS OF
ACCOUNTING FIRMS

Two accounting partners with international experience were asked to read the results of the full-scale study; later, they were interviewed to discuss the findings and results.

The two professional accountants found the findings interesting, and neither of them questioned the validity of this study. One of them was interested in learning that the systems' authority of Japanese firms was more decentralized than that of the U.S. firms. He corroborated the finding that Japanese firms put more emphasis on devaluation and revaluation of foreign currencies because Japanese companies usually handle more international transactions than U.S. companies.

The other accountant was surprised that about 32 percent of the U.S. firms allowed their divisions to purchase intermediate products from outside sources with complete freedom and 55 percent of the firms allowed outside purchases with the approval of the parent companies. He thought that the purchasing policies of U.S. firms were more restrictive than was found in this study.

NONRESPONSE BIAS TEST

A test was conducted to determine whether there was any significant nonresponse bias in the study. Respondents from the two national groups were further divided into two subgroups: early respondents and respondents to follow-up letters (late respondents). Late respondents were assumed to hold views similar to those of nonrespondents.[20] A comparison of the responses from the two subgroups was made by means of the chi-square test of homogeneity for each of the two national groups. The test was conducted for most questions included in the questionnaire.

The test results show that the early U.S. respondents held views similar to those of the late U.S. respondents and that there were no significant differences between the characteristics of the two U.S. subgroups. The test also shows that the early Japanese respondents had opinions similar to those of the late Japanese respondents. It was found that the percentage of Japanese MNCs in the early respondent group was higher than that of the late respondent group. Of the 38 early Japanese respondents, 34 were MNCs, whereas 41 of the 64 late respondents were MNCs. However, there were no significant differences in other characteristics, such as total revenue, amounts of exports to or imports from foreign subsidiaries, and percentage of interdivisional transfer.

SUMMARY

Findings and results of environmental variables and other issues were presented in this chapter. The findings indicate that the three most important environmental variables considered by the U.S. firms in formulating their international transfer pricing policies are the overall profits to the company, restrictions on repatriation of profits or dividends, and the competitive position of subsidiaries in foreign countries. Besides these three variables, Japanese companies also placed great importance on devaluation and revaluation of foreign currencies.

The results from a t test of the ratings by both groups on all 20 variables indicated that there were significant differences between their ratings on 10 of the 20 variables. The two most noticeable differences between the two groups were found in their ratings on two variables: the interests of local partners in foreign subsidiaries, and devaluation and revaluation in countries where the company has operations.

The key objectives of U.S. and Japanese transfer pricing systems appear to be quite similar. Maximizing consolidated profits and determining divisional performance were the two key objectives reported by most respondent firms in the two national groups.

The authority of determining transfer pricing policies among Japanese firms was more decentralized than that of U.S. firms; however, the outside purchasing policies of these Japanese firms were found to be more restrictive than those of the U.S. firms.

These findings were discussed with two practicing CPAs who have extensive international experience. Neither of the two questioned the validity of this research. Finally, a nonresponse bias test showed that late respondents held views similar to those of the early respondents.

NOTES

1. See Jeffrey S. Arpan, International Intracorporate Pricing: Non-American Systems and Views (New York: Praeger, 1972); James Greene and Michael G. Duerr, Intercompany Transactions in the Multinational Firm (New York: The Conference Board, 1970); and James S. Shulman, "When the Price Is Wrong—By Design," Columbia Journal of World Business 2 (May–June 1967): 69–76.

2. See Sidney Siegal, Nonparametric Statistics for the Behavioral Sciences (New York: McGraw-Hill, 1956), pp. 202-23.

3. Ernst & Ernst, Foreign Exchange Rates and Restrictions (New York: Ernst & Ernst, 1978), p. 3.

4. Ibid., p. 8.

5. See more examples in Shulman, op. cit., p. 72.

6. "Japan's Ways Thrive in the U.S.," Business Week, December 12, 1977, pp. 156, 160.

7. James S. Shulman, "Transfer Pricing in Multinational Business" (Ph.D. dissertation, Harvard University, 1966), p. 30.

8. See, for example, William M. Carley, "Profit Probes: Investigations Beset Multinational Firms with Stress on Pricing," Wall Street Journal, December 19, 1974, pp. 1, 20; and "UK Tax Authorities Zero in on Multinationals' Intercorporate Transfer Pricing," Business Europe, June 18, 1976, pp. 193-94.

9. "The U.N. May 'Audit' Business," Business Week, June 26, 1978, pp. 98, 100.

10. Shulman, "When the Price . . . ," p. 75.

11. Gordon Shillinglaw, Managerial Cost Accounting (Homewood, Ill.: Irwin, 1977), p. 851.

12. "Japan's Foreign Investments Continue to Soar as MITI Predicts Their Future Course," Business International, February 3, 1978, pp. 33-34.

13. "U.S. Total Direct Foreign Investment and Rates of Return, 1971-1976," Business International, October 14, 1977, pp. 324-25.

14. See M. Y. Yoshino, Japan's Multinational Enterprise (Cambridge, Mass.: Harvard University Press, 1976), pp. 127-59.

15. For an explanation of the t test of significance, see Norman H. Nie et al., Statistical Package for the Social Sciences (New York: McGraw-Hill, 1975), pp. 267-71.

16. Arpan, op. cit., p. 109.

17. Ibid., pp. 68-69.

18. R. L. Larson, "Decentralization in Real Life," Management Accounting 55 (March 1974):29.

19. See Howard F. Van Zandt, "How to Negotiate in Japan," Harvard Business Review 48 (November-December 1970):45; also see Peter F. Drucker, "What We Can Learn from Japanese Management," Harvard Business Review 49 (March-April 1971):111-13.

20. See evidence supporting the validity in A. N. Oppenheim, Questionnaire Design and Attitude Measurement (New York: Basic Books, 1966), p. 34.

7

SUMMARY AND CONCLUSIONS

This chapter summarizes the key aspects of the study, including research objectives and data collection procedure, major findings, results of hypotheses tested, and a summary of the similarities and differences between the two national groups. Qualifications and significant implications of the study will also be discussed. Suggestions for further research and general conclusions will be presented toward the end of the chapter.

SUMMARY OF THE RESEARCH

Objectives and Data Collection Procedure

The main objective of this research is to identify, measure, and explain the similarities and differences between transfer pricing practices in the United States and Japan. Information gathered by this study should provide guidance to large corporations in formulating their transfer pricing policies. The knowledge added by this research should improve future research and teaching in this area. Also, there are policy implications from this research for accounting-principles-setting bodies. The details of these implications will be discussed later.

Empirical data were gathered through a questionnaire survey that was carried out in two stages: a pilot study and a full-scale study. The results of the pilot study showed that a study based on larger samples was feasible. Therefore, a full-scale study was implemented using the revised questionnaire. Copies of the questionnaire were sent to a systematic sample of 300 U.S. firms. Questionnaires were also mailed to 369 Japanese firms not covered by the pilot study. The total number of usable responses was 247, which represented an overall usable response rate of 37 percent.

Two CPAs with international experience were asked to review the report of the full-scale study as a means of guarding against the drawing of unreasonable conclusions. These two professional accountants were associated with two international accounting firms.

Major Findings

Not only were the respondent firms in the two national groups comparable in terms of size, but over 80 percent of the respondents in both groups were MNCs and had comparable percentages of interdivisional transfers. Canada, the United Kingdom, and the German Federal Republic accounted for the greater amounts of exports to and imports from foreign subsidiaries by the U.S. firms. A large percentage of Japanese companies traded most of their products with their U.S. subsidiaries.

About 60 percent of the U.S. and Japanese respondent firms had interdivisional transfers of 10 percent or less of their total revenue. Around 30 percent of the respondent firms had intracompany transfers equivalent to 10-40 percent of their total revenue.

Transfer Pricing Methods

The use of transfer prices was more widespread among the U.S. firms than the Japanese firms. Of the U.S. firms, 92 percent used some form of transfer price, but only 73 percent of the Japanese companies did. Insignificant volume of interdivisional transfers was cited by a substantial majority of nonpricing companies as the main reason for not using transfer prices.

The more popular domestic transfer pricing methods used by U.S. firms were market price, full-production cost-plus, negotiated price, and standard full-production cost. The methods frequently used by Japanese companies to account for their domestic intracompany transfers included full-production cost-plus, negotiated price, market price, market price less selling expenses, and standard full-production cost. Many respondents used two or more domestic transfer prices.

Full-production cost-plus was found to be the most popular international transfer price among both the U.S. and the Japanese firms. A comparison between the dominant domestic transfer prices and dominant international transfer prices used by the U.S. and Japanese respondent firms showed that there was a significantly greater use of full-production cost-plus as the dominant international transfer prices among the respondents. Both the U.S. and Japanese international transfer prices were less cost-oriented than were their domestic transfer prices.

The use of the marginal cost concept and mathematical programming was found to be very limited among the respondents. The decomposition method, linear programming, and other methods frequently discussed by academic writers were not mentioned by any of the respondent firms.

Environmental Variables

The respondents were asked to rate the importance of 20 environmental variables usually considered by multinational firms in formulating their international transfer pricing policies. The rating was done on a scale of one (not at all important) to five (extremely important). An analysis of the ratings showed that "overall profit to the company" was given the highest mean rating by both the Japanese and the U.S. subject groups. Other variables to which high ratings were given by the two groups include restrictions on repatriation of profits and dividends, competitive position of foreign subsidiaries, and performance evaluation of foreign subsidiaries.

Statistical tests showed that there was some agreement on the relative importance (or rank order) of the 20 variables between Japanese and U.S. respondents. However, there were significant differences between the absolute importance (mean rating) placed upon 10 of the 20 variables by the two national groups.

System Objectives and Other Policies

The key objectives for transfer pricing systems of the U.S. and Japanese firms appear to be quite similar. Maximizing consolidated profits and determining divisional performances were the two most important objectives reported by the respondents in both groups.

The process of determining transfer pricing policies was found to be primarily a centralized function handled by executives of the parent companies. Relatively speaking, the policy-formulating process among Japanese companies was more decentralized than that of the U.S. firms.

A comparison of the ways in which policy disagreements among divisions were settled by the respondent firms showed that a majority of the U.S. companies' divisional disagreements were settled by financial executives from the parent companies, whereas most Japanese firms resolved their disagreements through negotiation among divisions. An analysis of the policies on outside purchasing of raw materials and intermediate products indicated that the policies of Japanese companies were more restrictive than those of U.S. firms.

Interviews with CPAs and Nonresponse Bias Test

Two experienced CPAs were interviewed to discuss the findings and results. The two accountants found the findings interesting, and neither questioned the validity of the research. A nonresponse bias test indicated that there were similar views between early respondents and late respondents on most questions asked in the questionnaire.

HYPOTHESES TESTED

Seven hypotheses were tested in this study. The following paragraphs summarize the results of these tests.

Hypothesis A-1 states that the extent of application of cost-oriented or non-cost-oriented domestic transfer prices among LAIC and LJIC does not vary according to the nationality of these firms. This hypothesis was not rejected by the chi-square test, indicating that there was no significant difference between the orientations of the domestic transfer prices used by LAIC and LJIC.

Hypothesis A-2 states that the extent of application of cost-oriented or non-cost-oriented international transfer prices among LAIC and LJIC does not vary according to the nationality of these companies. This hypothesis was also not rejected by the chi-square test. It shows that there was no significant difference in the orientations of the international transfer prices used by the U.S. and Japanese respondent firms.

From the test results of hypotheses A-1 and A-2, it can be concluded that U.S. transfer pricing systems are neither distinctly more cost-oriented nor distinctly more non-cost-oriented than Japanese systems. This conclusion is important because it directly refutes one of Arpan's conclusions for U.S. and Japanese firms, namely:

> U.S. systems of international intracorporate pricing
> are distinctly more cost oriented and more complex
> than non-U.S. systems.[1]

The above discrepancy may have resulted from the fact that Arpan's study was based on the answers from 60 U.S. subsidiaries of foreign firms and interviews with eight CPAs, whereas this research was based on the response from the parent companies of 145 U.S. and 102 Japanese industrial corporations.

Hypothesis B-1 states that the extent of usage of cost-oriented transfer prices for domestic interdivisional transfers among LAIC is not related to the size of these companies. The hypothesis was not rejected by the test. This suggests that there is no relationship between size and the extent of usage of cost-oriented domestic transfer price among U.S. firms.

Hypothesis B-2 states that the extent of usage of cost-oriented transfer prices for <u>domestic</u> interdivisional transfers among LJIC is not related to the size of these companies. This hypothesis was rejected by the chi-square test. An examination of data reported by the Japanese firms show that the larger the size of the Japanese company, the more likely will be the use of a non-cost-oriented domestic transfer price.

Hypothesis B-3 states that the extent of usage of cost-oriented transfer prices for <u>international</u> interdivisional transfers among LAIC is not related to the size of these companies. The hypothesis was not rejected by the chi-square test. This indicates that the extent of usage of cost-oriented international transfer prices among the U.S. firms is not related to the size of these companies.

Hypothesis B-4 states that the extent of usage of cost-oriented transfer prices for <u>international</u> interdivisional transfers among LJIC is not related to the size of these companies. The statistical test rejected hypothesis B-4. An investigation of the data reported by Japanese firms showed that the larger the size of the Japanese firm, the more likely is the use of non-cost-oriented international transfer price.

From the test results of hypotheses B-1, B-2, B-3, and B-4, it is concluded that there is no significant relationship between the size of large U.S. industrial firms and the use of cost-oriented transfer prices among these companies. However, there is a significant relationship between the size of large Japanese industrial firms and the use of non-cost-oriented transfer price among these Japanese corporations, that is, the larger the size of the Japanese firm, the more likely will be the use of non-cost-oriented transfer prices. This conclusion is significant because it contradicts yet another of Arpan's findings, which stated:

> There is a substantial correlation between the firm's size and the transfer pricing system orientation: the larger the parent firm, the more likely it is to use a cost-oriented system . . . .[2]

Hypothesis C-1 states that there is no significant difference between the absolute importance placed upon each of the major environmental variables by LAIC and LJIC when they formulate their international transfer pricing policies. Data reported by respondents on environmental variables were used to test the hypothesis. A substantial majority of the companies that provided answers to the section on environmental variables were MNCs. A t test shows that hypothesis C-1 was rejected for 10 of the 20 variables. There were significant differences between the absolute importance given to these 10 variables by the two subject groups. Noticeable differences between the two groups were found in their ratings on two variables: devaluation and revaluation of foreign currencies, and the interests of local partners in foreign subsidiaries. The above conclusion gives very little support to one of Arpan's conclusions, namely, that the very large MNCs of all nationalities exhibit the smallest differences in views of attendant problems.[3]

SIMILARITIES AND DIFFERENCES
BETWEEN THE TWO NATIONAL GROUPS

Now that we have reviewed the study in summary form, it may be useful to have an overview of the similarities and differences between the transfer pricing practices of U.S. and Japanese firms. These similarities and differences are summarized in Table 7.1, which may enable us to visualize some of the unique features and strengths of the transfer pricing systems in each of the two countries. A closer attention and better understanding of the systems and practices of other countries may point the way to better solutions to many of our problems in transfer pricing.

QUALIFICATIONS

When assessing the results and accepting the conclusions of the study, readers should recognize some of the limitations of this research. First, the response rate of Japanese firms was 30 percent, which was lower than that of the U.S. firms. This may have caused an unknown bias undetected by the nonresponse bias tests.

Second, the questionnaire was printed in English only. Although efforts were made to remove the ambiguities and any possible misunderstanding of the terms used in the questionnaire, there is no guarantee that the Japanese interpretations of the important terms were the same as those of U.S. firms.

Third, questionnaires to the U.S. firms were mailed to the controller, treasurer, financial vice-president, or secretary (preference given in that order) of the firms, whereas questionnaires to the Japanese companies were mailed to the presidents of these companies. This difference in treatment may have created another unknown bias in the study.

TABLE 7.1: Similarities and Differences between the Transfer Pricing Practices
of the U.S. and Japanese Firms

Similarities	Differences
Systems' objectives: The two major objectives reported by both national groups were maximizing consolidated profits and determining divisional performances.	The extent of usage of transfer price(s): The use of transfer prices among U.S. firms is more extensive than in Japanese companies.
Systems' orientation: There was no significant difference between the system orientation of both groups.	System authority: The systems' authority of U.S. firms was more centralized than that of Japanese firms.
Perception of the relative importance of major environmental variables: Both groups had some agreement on the relative importance of the 20 variables.	Ways of settlement of policy disagreements: Policy disagreements among divisions are settled mainly by parent company executives in U.S. firms; but Japanese resolve their disagreements mainly through negotiation.
	The absolute importance of major environmental variables: There were significant differences between the ratings of the two groups on 10 of the 20 variables.
	Outside purchasing policies: The outside purchasing policies of Japanese are more restrictive than those of U.S. firms.

Source: Compiled by the author.

Finally, the study sampled large U.S. and Japanese industrial firms. Technically, therefore, the conclusions apply only to large industrial firms in the United States and Japan. Care must be taken when generalizing the results to nonindustrial companies or to smaller firms.

IMPLICATIONS

There are several implications of this study for financial management, for educators and researchers on transfer pricing, and for accounting-principles-setting bodies. Some of the more obvious implications are discussed in the following paragraphs.

Implications for Financial Management

As pointed out in previous chapters, there are many environmental variables related to international transfer pricing and they are constantly changing. It may be difficult if not impossible for a multinational firm to find an optimal transfer price or design a transfer policy that takes all these variables into consideration. However, the information on ranking of the 20 environmental variables in Table 6.1 may provide some guidance for firms trying to establish their international transfer pricing policies for the first time or for companies in the process of revising their policies. The following summarizes that five most important variables considered by the U.S. and Japanese respondents in formulating their transfer pricing policies:

Five variables most important to U.S. firms	Five variables most important to Japanese firms
Profit consideration	Profit consideration
Restrictions on repatriation of profits or dividends	Competitive position of foreign subsidiaries
Competitive position of foreign subsidiaries	Devaluation and revaluation of foreign currencies
Differentials in income tax rates and income tax legislation among countries	Restrictions on repatriation of profits or dividends
Divisional performance evaluation	Divisional performance evaluation

Implications for Educators and Researchers
on Transfer Pricing

As a result of this study, educators and students in international accounting and comparative management are provided, for the first time in English literature, extensive statistical evidence of Japanese transfer pricing practices. Current information on U.S. transfer pricing systems is also supplied by this research. This will contribute to a better understanding of management approaches in a variety of environments. If researchers and educators are to generate a body of theory on transfer pricing and to make the theory more general and valid, the type of cross-national information provided by this study is essential.

Another implication of this report is the invitation to replicate both Arpan's and this author's studies. Arpan's research was considered to be one of the most authoritative studies in international transfer pricing. However, the results of this study provide very little support for many of Arpan's conclusions. Thus, further research is needed to test both Arpan's and this author's conclusions.

Finally, an important implication for researchers is that there is a gap between the methods and concepts advocated by many writers, and those of practitioners with respect to the use of transfer prices. The concepts of marginal cost, the decomposition method, and linear programming have been advocated by many authorities in the past but the application of these concepts and methods appears to be rather limited. The impact of research on transfer pricing practices done by these writers has been minimal. Additional research is needed to narrow the gap between researchers and practitioners.

Implications for Accounting-Principle-
Setting Bodies

In Chapter 3 it was reported that some Japanese companies used transfer prices to smooth their earnings or to make the parent-only statements look good. J. A. Milburn also found that the reporting results of major Canadian companies were highly sensitive to international transfer pricing variability.[4]

To reduce the abuses on transfer pricing and on related party transactions, the American Institute of Certified Public Accountants (AICPA) established extensive disclosure requirements on related party transactions.[5] However, there are no similar requirements in most other countries.

Intracompany transactions have become increasingly important for many companies. There seems to be a great temptation for some firms to smooth their earnings through transfer prices. In order to protect investors, accounting-principle-setting bodies should establish comprehensive disclosure requirements on related party transactions.

SUGGESTIONS FOR FURTHER RESEARCH

This study examines only some of the facets of transfer pricing. Further research needs to be done in many areas of transfer pricing, especially international transfer pricing.

To understand more about the views of non-U.S. systems, studies could be done using the parent companies of European industrial companies or Latin American industrial companies as subjects. The results of such a study could then be compared with the findings and conclusions described in this book.

As mentioned in Chapter 6 and in this chapter, most LJIC settled their policy disagreements mainly through negotiation among the divisions involved. Studies could be done to investigate the conflict resolution process of these companies. Such research might be done through in-depth interviews with executives in a number of large Japanese firms.

To know more about U.S. views of transfer pricing, studies might be done on transfer pricing practices of foreign subsidiaries of U.S. firms. This type of study has been suggested by James S. Shulman "to compare actual practices abroad with perceived goals at home."[6]

Current value accounting and price-level adjusted statements have been advocated by many authorities, and the former is now under consideration in many countries. If this system is adopted, many aspects of transfer pricing will take on new dimensions. Studies exploring the feasibility of using current value as a transfer pricing method would appear to be appropriate and should yield valuable information.

GENERAL CONCLUSIONS

Several general conclusions can be drawn from the study. First, a majority of Japanese and U.S. respondents considered transfer pricing, especially international transfer pricing, to be one of the most important corporate functions, vital to the company's profits and the evaluation of divisional performances. This trend is likely to continue in the future. The problems of transfer pricing will increase in magnitude and complexity, mainly because of the following factors:

Large multinational enterprises are expanding their foreign investments.

International trade, which consists a large amount of transfers between related business entities, will continue to increase in the foreseeable future.

Tax and customs authorities of many countries will intensify their surveillance on the transfer pricing practices of MNCs.

The second general conclusion relates to the design and administration of a transfer pricing system. The broad policy and ultimate goals of the system should be clear and consistent so that the company is less vulnerable to attacks by government authorities. However, in maneuvering the system, sufficient flexibility must be retained to alleviate many potential problems and to respond to major changes in the international environment.

Finally, the abundance of existing research in this area confirms that many researchers were addressing their research to one of the most pressing problems in the business world. However, until now a substantial amount of the research focused on the merits of various pricing proposals and other theoretical inquiries into the subject, such as building models and so forth. In the future, if researchers wish to provide useful guidance for practitioners, the topics of research must be diversified into other areas. Additional empirical studies are needed to analyze the transfer pricing problems facing MNCs.

NOTES

1. Jeffrey S. Arpan, International Intracorporate Pricing: Non-American Systems and Views (New York: Praeger, 1972), p. 109.

2. Ibid., p. 79.

3. Ibid., p. 109.

4. J. Alex Milburn, "International Transfer Transactions: What Price?" CA Magazine 109 (December 1976):26.

5. Statement on Auditing Standards No. 6, "Related Party Transactions" (New York: American Institute of Certified Public Accountants, 1975), pp. 9-10.

6. James S. Shulman, "Transfer Pricing in Multinational Business" (Ph.D. dissertation, Harvard University, 1966), p. 153.

BIBLIOGRAPHY

BOOKS AND MONOGRAPHS

Aggarwal, Raj. Financial Policies for the Multinational Company. New York: Praeger, 1976.

Amey, L. R., and D. A. Egginton. Management Accounting, A Conceptual Approach. London: Longman, 1973.

Anthony, Robert N., and James S. Reece. Management Accounting, Text and Cases. Fifth ed. Homewood, Ill.: Irwin, 1975.

Arpan, Jeffrey S. International Intracorporate Pricing: Non-American Systems and Views. New York: Praeger, 1972.

Ballon, Robert J., Iwao Tomita, and Hajime Usami. Financial Reporting in Japan. Tokyo: Kodansha International, 1976.

Bierman, Harold, Jr., and Thomas R. Dyckman. Managerial Cost Accounting. Second ed. New York: MacMillan, 1976.

Business International Corporation. Setting Intercorporate Pricing. New York: BIC, 1973.

Business International Corporation. Solving International Pricing Problems. New York, 1965.

Cateora, Philip R., and John M. Hess. International Marketing. Third ed. Homewood, Ill.: Irwin, 1975.

Choi, Frederick D. S., and Gerhard G. Mueller. An Introduction to Multinational Accounting. Englewood Cliffs, N.J.: Prentice-Hall, 1978.

Conoven, W. J. Practical Nonparametric Statistics. New York: John Wiley and Sons, 1971.

Denison, Edward F., and William K. Chung. How Japan's Economy Grew So Fast. Washington, D.C.: The Brookings Institution, 1976.

Duerr, Michael G. Tax Allocations and International Business. New York: The Conference Board, 1972.

____. The Problems Facing International Management. New York: The Conference Board, 1974.

Ernst & Ernst. A Digest of Principal Taxes in Japan. New York: Ernst & Ernst, 1975.

____. Foreign and U.S. Corporate Income and Withholding Tax Rates. Cleveland, Ohio: Ernst & Ernst, 1978.

Fayerweather, John. International Business Management: A Conceptual Framework. New York: McGraw-Hill, 1969.

Frank, Isaiah, ed. The Japanese Economy in International Perspective. Baltimore, Md.: Johns Hopkins University Press, 1975.

____, and Ryokichi Hirono, eds. How the United States and Japan See Each Other's Economy. New York: Committee for Economic Development, 1974.

Fukuda, Haruko. Japan and World Trade: The Years Ahead. Lexington, Mass.: Lexington Books, 1973.

Greene, James, and Michael G. Duerr. Intercompany Transactions in the Multinational Firm. New York: The Conference Board, 1970.

Haskin & Sells. Taxation in Japan. New York: Haskins & Sells, 1977.

Hayashi, Taizo. Guide to Japanese Taxes 1977-78. Tokyo: Zaikei Shōhō Sha, 1977.

Horngren, Charles T. Cost Accounting: A Managerial Emphasis. Fourth ed. Englewood Cliffs, N.J.: Prentice-Hall, 1977.

Mautz, Robert K. Financial Reporting by Diversified Companies. New York: Financial Executives Research Foundation, 1968.

Moore, Russell M., and George M. Scott, eds. An Introduction to Financial Control and Reporting in Multinational Enterprises. Studies in International Business No. 1. Austin, Texas: Bureau of Business Research, The University of Texas at Austin, 1973.

National Association of Accountants. Accounting for Intracompany Transfers. Research Series No. 30. New York: National Association of Accountants, 1956.

____. Management Accounting Problems in Foreign Operations. Research Report 36. New York: National Association of Accountants, 1960.

National Industrial Conference Board. Interdivisional Transfer Pricing. Studies in Business Policy No. 122. New York: The Conference Board, 1967.

____. Managing the International Financial Function. Studies in Business Policy No. 133. New York: The Conference Board, 1970.

Nie, Norman H., H. C. Hull, J. G. Jenkens, K. Steinbrenner, and D. H. Bent. Statistical Package for the Social Sciences. New York: McGraw-Hill, 1975.

Nieckels, Lars. Transfer Pricing in Multinational Firms, a Heuristic Programming Approach and a Case Study. Stockholm, Sweden: Almqvist and Wiksell International, 1976.

Norbury, Paul, and Geoffrey Bownas, eds. Business in Japan. New York: John Wiley and Sons, 1974.

Oppenheim, A. N. Questionnaire Design and Attitude Measurement. New York: Basic Books, 1966.

Price Waterhouse. Corporate Taxes in 80 Countries. New York, 1978.

Robbins, Sidney M., and Robert B. Stobaugh. Money in the Multinational Enterprise, a Study of Financial Policy. New York: Basic Books, 1973.

Robock, Stefan H., Kenneth Simmonds, and Jack Zwick. International Business and Multinational Enterprises. Homewood, Ill.: Irwin, 1977.

Shillinglaw, Gordon. Managerial Cost Accounting. Fourth ed. Homewood, Ill.: Irwin, 1977.

Siegal, Sidney. Nonparametric Statistics for the Behavioral Sciences. New York: McGraw-Hill, 1956.

Solomons, David. Divisional Performance: Measurement and Control. Homewood, Ill.: Irwin, 1965.

Tsurumi, Yoshi. The Japanese Are Coming. Cambridge, Mass.: Ballinger, 1976.

Verlage, H. C. Transfer Pricing for Multinational Enterprises. Rotterdam, Netherlands: Rotterdam University Press, 1975.

Weston, J. Fred, and Bart W. Sorge. International Managerial Finance. Homewood, Ill.: Irwin, 1972.

Yoshino, M. Y. Japan's Managerial System, Tradition and Innovation. Cambridge, Mass.: MIT Press, 1968.

____. The Japanese Marketing System: Adaptations and Innovations. Cambridge, Mass.: MIT Press, 1971.

____. Marketing in Japan. New York: Praeger, 1975.

____. Japan's Multinational Enterprises. Cambridge, Mass.: Harvard University Press, 1976.

Zenoff, David B., and Jack Zwick. International Financial Management. Englewood Cliffs, N.J.: Prentice-Hall, 1969.

ARTICLES AND PERIODICALS

Abdel-Khalik, Rashad, and Edward J. Lusk. "Transfer Pricing— A Synthesis." Accounting Review 49 (January 1974): 8-23.

Anthony, Robert N. "Some Fruitful Directions for Research in Management Accounting." In Accounting Research 1960-1970: A Critical Evaluation, pp. 37-68. Edited by Nicholas Dopuch and Lawrence Revsine. Center for International Education and Research in Accounting, University of Illinois at Urbana-Champaign, 1973.

Arpan, Jeffrey S. "International Intracorporate Pricing: Non-American Systems and Views." Journal of International Business Studies 3 (Spring 1972): 1-18.

Arrow, K. J. "Optimization, Decentralization, and Internal Pricing in Business Firms." In Contributions to Scientific Research in

Management, pp. 9-17. Los Angeles: University of California at Los Angeles, 1959.

Bailey, Andrew D. Jr., and Warren J. Boe. "Goal and Resource Transfers in the Multigoal Organization." Accounting Review 51 (July 1976): 559-73.

Baumol, William J., and Tibor Fabian. "Decomposition, Pricing for Decentralization and External Economics." Management Science 11 (September 1964): 1-32.

Bernhard, Richard H. "Some Problems in Applying Mathematical Programming to Opportunity Cost." Journal of Accounting Research 6 (Spring 1968): 143-48.

Bierman, Harold, Jr. "Pricing Intracompany Transfer." Accounting Review 34 (July 1959): 429-32.

Boyd, Robert. "Transfer Prices and Profitability Measurement." The Controller 29 (February 1961): 88-89.

Boyer, J. R. "Intracorporate Pricing Effect on ROI Analysis." Financial Executive 32 (December 1964): 20, 22-23, 26.

Brantner, Paul F. "Taxation and the Multinational Firm." Management Accounting 55 (October 1973): 11-16, 26.

Carley, William M. "Profit Probes: Investigations Beset Multinational Firms with Stress on Pricing." Wall Street Journal, December 19, 1974, pp. 1, 20.

Chasteen, L. G. "Shadow Prices: A Graphical Approach." Management Accounting 54 (September 1972): 27-29.

Cook, Paul W. "Decentralization and Transfer-Price Problem." Journal of Business 28 (April 1955): 87-94.

Dantzig, George, and Philip Wolfe. "Decomposition Principle for Linear Programming." Operations Research 8 (January-February 1960): 101-11.

Dascher, Paul E. "Transfer Pricing—Some Behavioral Observations." Managerial Planning 21 (November-December 1972): 17-21.

Day, C. F. "Shadow Prices for Evaluation Alternative Uses of Available Capacity." NAA Bulletin 40 (May 1959): 67-76.

Dean, Joel. "Decentralization and Intracompany Pricing." Harvard Business Review 33 (July–August 1955): 65–74.

____. "Profit Performance Measurement of Division Managers." The Controller 25 (September 1957): 423–24, 426, 449.

Dearden, John. "Interdivisional Pricing." Harvard Business Review 38 (January–February 1960): 117–25.

Dittman, David A. "Transfer Pricing and Decentralization." Management Accounting 54 (November 1972): 47–50.

Dopuch, Nicholoas, and David E. Drake. "Accounting Implications of a Mathematical Programming Approach to the Transfer Price Problem." Journal of Accounting Research 2 (Spring 1964): 10–24.

Drebin, Allen R. "A Proposal for Dual Pricing of Intracompany Transfers." NAA Bulletin 40 (February 1959): 51–55.

Drucker, Peter F. "What We Can Learn from Japanese Management." Harvard Business Review 49 (March–April 1971): 111–13.

Edwards, James Don, and Roger A. Roemmich. "Transfer Pricing: The Wrong Tool for Performance Evaluation," Cost and Management 50 (January–February 1976): 35–37.

Emmanuel, Clive. "Transfer Pricing: A Diagnosis and Possible Solution to Dysfunctional Decision-Making in the Divisionalized Company." Management International Review 17 (1977/4): 45–59.

Fantl, Irving L. "Transfer Pricing—Tread Carefully." CPA Journal 44 (December 1974): 42–46.

Finney, Frederick D. "Pricing Interdivisional Transfers." Management Accounting 48 (November 1966): 10–18.

Fremgen, James M. "Transfer Pricing and Management Goal." Management Accounting 52 (December 1970): 25–31.

Goetz, Billy E. "Transfer Prices: An Exercise in Relevancy and Goal Congruence." Accounting Review 42 (July 1967): 435–70.

Gordon, Myron J. "A Method of Pricing for a Socialist Economy." Accounting Review 45 (July 1970): 427–43.

Gould, J. R. "Internal Pricing in Firms—When There Are Costs of Using an Outside Market." Journal of Business 37 (January 1964): 61-67.

Greene, James. "Intercompany Pricing Across National Frontiers." Conference Board Record 6 (October 1969): 43-48.

Greer, Howard C. "Divisional Profit Calculation, Notes on the 'Transfer Rate' Problem." NAA Bulletin 43 (July 1962): 5-12.

Gregory, Gene. "Japan's New Multinationalism: The Cannon Giessen Experience." Columbia Journal of World Business 11 (Spring 1976): 122-29.

Haidinger, Timothy P. "Negotiate for Profits." Management Accounting 52 (December 1970): 23-24, 52.

Hass, J. E. "Transfer Pricing in a Decentralized Firm." Management Science 14 (February 1968): B310-B333.

Hirshleifer, Jack. "On the Economics of Transfer Pricing." Journal of Business 29 (July 1956): 172-84.

____. "Economics of the Divisionalized Firm." Journal of Business 30 (April 1957): 96-108.

Holstrum, Gary L., and E. H. Sauls. "The Opportunity Cost Transfer Price." Management Accounting 54 (May 1973): 29-33.

Holzman, R. S. "IRS Amplifies Rules for Intercompany Transactions." Management Review 57 (July 1968): 37-41.

"The Japanese Economy Today and U.S.-Japan Economic Relations." Business Week, July 24, 1978, pp. 16, 18, 20-21, 23-25.

"Japan's Accounting Shake-up," Business Week, April 25, 1977, p. 114.

"Japan's Foreign Investments Continue to Soar as MITI Predicts Their Future Course." Business International, February 3, 1978, pp. 33-34.

"Japan's Ways Thrive in the U.S." Business Week, December 12, 1977, pp. 156, 160.

Keegen, W. J. "Multinational Pricing: How Far is Arm's-Length?" Columbia Journal of World Business 4 (May-June 1969):57-66.

Kraar, Louis. "Japan's Great Buying Offensive." Fortune, April 24, 1978, pp. 42-44.

Larson, Raymond L. "Decentralization in Real Life." Management Accounting 55 (March 1974):28-32.

Lemke, Kenneth W. "In Defence of the 'Profit Center' Concept." Abacus 6 (December 1970):182-88.

Li, David H. "Interdivisional Transfer Planning." Management Accounting 46 (June 1965):51-54.

MacGregor, Douglas. "An Uneasy Look at Performance Appraisal." Harvard Business Review 35 (May-June 1957):89-94.

Malmstron, Duane. "Accommodating Exchange Rate Fluctuations in Intercompany Pricing and Invoicing." Management Accounting 59 (September 1977):24-28.

Matsuoka, Iwaki. "Comparative Management and Management in Japan." Management Japan 6 (Autumn 1972):34-38.

Milburn, J. Alex. "International Transfer Transactions: What Price?" CA Magazine 109 (December 1976):22-27.

Nagy, Richard J. "Transfer Price Accounting for MNCs." Management Accounting 59 (January 1978):34-38.

Negandhi, Anant R. "Cross-Cultural Management Studies: Too Many Conclusions, Not Enough Conceptualization." Management International Review 14 (1974/6):59-72.

O'Connor, Walter F. "Intercompany Pricing in Foreign Operation." Management Controls 13 (July 1966):144-49.

Onsi, Mohamed. "A Transfer Pricing System Based on Opportunity Cost." Accounting Review 45 (July 1970):535-43.

____. "Transfer Pricing System Based on Opportunity Costs: A Reply." Accounting Review 49 (January 1974):129-31.

Pascale, Richard T. "Communication and Decision Making across Cultures: Japanese and American Comparisons." Administrative Science Quarterly 23 (March 1978): 91-110.

Petty, J. W. II, and Ernest W. Walker. "Optimal Transfer Pricing for the Multinational Firm." Financial Management 1 (Winter 1972): 74-84.

Piper, A. G. "Internal Trading." Accountancy 80 (October 1969): 733-36.

Reece, James S., and William R. Cool. "Measuring Investment Center Performance." Harvard Business Review 56 (May-June 1978): 28-30, 34, 36, 40, 42, 46, 174, 176.

Ronen, J., and G. McKinney. "Transfer Pricing for Divisional Autonomy." Journal of Accounting Research 8 (Spring 1970): 99-112.

Rutenberg, David P. "Maneuvering Liquid Assets in a Multinational Company: Formulation and Deterministic Solution Procedures." Management Science 16 (June 1970): B671-B683.

Samuels, J. M. "Opportunity Costing: An Application of Mathematical Programming." Journal of Accounting Research 3 (Autumn 1965): 182-91.

Satta, Kazutoshi. "How a Japanese Trading Company Operates." Japan Report 23 (March 16, 1977): 5-6.

Schwab, Richard J. "A Contribution Approach To Transfer Pricing." Management Accounting 56 (February 1975): 46-48.

Seghers, Paul D. "How to Set and Defend Intercompany Prices Under Section 482 Regulations." Taxes 47 (October 1969): 606-22.

Sharav, Itzhak. "Transfer Pricing—Diversity of Goals and Practices." Journal of Accountancy 137 (April 1974): 56-62.

Shaub, H. James. "Transfer Pricing in a Decentralized Organization." Management Accounting 59 (April 1978): 33-36, 42.

Shillinglaw, Gordon. "Guides to Internal Profit Measurement." Harvard Business Review 35 (March-April 1957): 82-94.

____. "Problems in Divisional Profit Measurement." NAA Bulletin 42 (March 1961): 33-43.

____. "Toward a Theory of Divisional Income Measurement." Accounting Review 37 (April 1962): 208-16.

Shulman, James S. "When the Price is Wrong—By Design." Columbia Journal of World Business 2 (May-June 1967): 69-76.

____. "Transfer Pricing in the Multinational Firm." In International Marketing Strategy, pp. 312-22. Edited by H. B. Thorelli. Baltimore, Md.: Penguin, 1973.

Solomons, David. "Intra Corporate Conflict in International Business." In Topics in Accounting and Planning, pp. 1-15. Edited by Richard Mattessich. Vancouver, Canada: University of British Columbia, 1972.

Stanley, Curtis H. "Cost-Basis Valuations in Transactions Between Entities." Accounting Review 39 (July 1964): 639-47.

Stewart, J. C. "Multinational Companies and Transfer Pricing." Journal of Business Finance and Accounting 4 (Autumn 1977): 353-71.

Stitt, Hubert, and John Connor. "International Intercompany Pricing." Canadian Tax Journal 10 (March-April 1962): 85-92.

Stone, W. E. "Intercompany Pricing." Accounting Review 31 (October 1956): 625-27.

____. "Tax Consideration in Intra-Company Pricing." Accounting Review 35 (January 1960): 45-58.

____. "Legal Implications of Intracompany Pricing." Accounting Review 39 (January 1964): 38-42.

Taira, Koji. "Reflections on U.S.-Japan Economic Conflict." Management Japan 6 (Winter 1973): 26-34.

Talwar, Akshay K. "Transfer Pricing System Based on Opportunity Costs: A Comment." Accounting Review 49 (January 1974): 126-31.

Thomas, Arthur L. "Transfer Prices of the Multinational Firm: When Will They Be Arbitrary?" Abacus 7 (June 1971): 40-53.

Troxel, Richard B. "On Transfer Pricing." CPA Journal 43 (October 1973): 895-97.

Tsurumi, Yoshi. "Critical Choice for Japan: Cooperation or Conflict with the United States." Columbia Journal of World Business 12 (Spring 1977): 14-20.

"The U.N. May 'Audit' Business." Business Week, June 26, 1978, pp. 98, 100.

Van Zandt, Howard F. "How to Negotiate in Japan." Harvard Business Review 48 (November-December 1970): 45-56.

Vendig, R. E. "A Three-Part Transfer Price." Management Accounting 55 (September 1973): 33-36.

Walter, J. T. "Eli Lilly Decision." Taxes 45 (September 1967): 622-24.

Watson, David J. H., and John V. Baumler. "Transfer Pricing: A Behavioral Context." Accounting Review 50 (July 1975): 466-74.

Wells, M. C. "Profit Centers, Transfer Prices and Mysticism." Abacus 4 (December 1968): 174-81.

_____. "Transfer Prices and Profit Center? No," Abacus 7 (June 1971): 54-57.

Whinston, Andrew. "Pricing Guides in Decentralized Organizations." In New Perspective in Organizational Research, pp. 405-48. Edited by W. W. Cooper, H. H. Leavitt, and M. W. Shelly. New York: John Wiley and Sons, 1964.

Wojdak, J. F. "Introduction to the External Aspects of Transfer-Pricing." New York Certified Public Accountant 38 (May 1968): 341-52.

OTHER SOURCES

Bisat, Talal A. "An Evaluation of International Intercompany Transactions." Ph.D. dissertation, American University, 1967.

The Business Accounting Principles Board of Japan, Renketsu Zaimu-Shoyō no Seido-ka ni Kansuru Iken-sho [Opinion on the

Systematization of Consolidated Financial Statements] (Tokyo: Business Accounting Principles Board, 1975).

Milburn, J. Alex. "International Transfer Pricing in a Financial Accounting Context." Ph.D. dissertation, University of Illinois at Urbana-Champaign, 1977.

The Ministry of Finance of Japan, Renketsu Zaimusyohyō Kisoku [Rules for Preparing Consolidated Financial Statements] (Tokyo: Ministry of Finance, 1976).

Okpechi, Simeon O. "Interdivisional Transfer-Pricing: A Conflict Resolution Approach." Ph.D. dissertation, The Ohio State University, 1976.

Petty, John W. "An Optimal Transfer-Pricing System for the Multinational Firm: A Linear-Programming Approach." Ph.D. dissertation, University of Texas at Austin, 1971.

Shulman, James S. "Transfer Pricing in Multinational Business." D.B.A. dissertation, Harvard University, 1966.

Stone, Willard E. "Management Practices With Respect to Internal Transfer Pricing in Large Manufacturing Companies." Ph.D. dissertation, University of Pennsylvania, 1957.

Tang, Roger Y. W., and K. H. Chan. "A Discriminant Analysis of International Transfer Pricing Policies in the United States and Japan." Paper presented at the Joint Statistical Meetings of the American Statistical Association, the Biometric Society, and the Institute of Mathematical Statistics, San Diego, August 14-17, 1978.

INDEX

American Institute of Certified
Public Accountants (AICPA):
disclosure requirements on
related party transactions,
107
American Respondents:
exports to foreign subsidiaries, 53; imports from
foreign subsidiaries, 54;
industrial classification, 48,
51; percentages of interdivisional transfers to total
revenue, 56; total revenue
of, 51-52; use of transfer
prices, 59, 60, 63
antidumping investigations:
in the United States, 34, 37;
in European Economic Com-
munity (EEC), 34;
antidumping legislation, 17
anti-monopoly and Fair Trade
Law of Japan, 29
antitrust legislation: 82; of
the United States, 29, 37; of
Japan, 37
Argentina, 83
Arpan, Jeffrey S., 4, 20, 22,
30, 72, 74, 75, 78, 88, 102,
104, 107
Australia, 55, 85

Baumol, W. J., 12
Bierman, Harold Jr., 13
Bisat, T. A., 19, 22
Business Accounting Principles
Board of Japan, 31
Business Asia, 35
Business International Corpora-
tion (BIC), 17, 21, 22

Canada, 53, 54, 57, 100
comparable uncontrolled price
method, 11
competitive position of foreign
subsidiaries, 82, 84, 97, 101
The Conference Board (see,
National Industrial Conference
Board)
consolidated financial statements,
31, 45
Cook, P. W., 11
customs duties, 17, 78, 92

Dean, Joel, 12
decomposition method (procedure),
4, 12, 64, 101, 107
devaluation: as an environmental
variable, 82, 85, 96, 97; of
the U.S. dollar (see, U.S.
dollar)
direct foreign investments: of
the United States, 53, 85; of
Japan, 37
Drebin, Allen R., 12
dual pricing (see, transfer prices)
Duerr, Michael G., 19, 22, 67,
78
dumping: 68; practices of Japanese firms, 34
dumping investigations (see, antidumping investigations)

Edwards, James Don, 12
Emmanuel, Clive, 17
environmental variables of transfer pricing, 5, 19, 78-79, 97,
101, 103-04, 106
European Economic Community
(EEC), 32, 34

ABOUT THE AUTHOR

ROGER Y. W. TANG is an Assistant Professor in the Faculty of Management at McGill University, Montreal, Canada. He received his Ph.D. in business administration from the University of Nebraska in 1977. He was born in mainland China, and has lived and worked in Burma, Thailand, Taiwan, the United States, and Canada.

Before joining McGill University, Dr. Tang taught accounting courses in the Department of Accounting at the University of Nebraska-Lincoln. He has also held positions in private business and served as a consultant to the Chinese Petroleum Corporation and Chung Tai Petrochemical Corporation in Taiwan.

Dr. Tang is the author of several articles on accounting and international business, and he has presented seminars in the areas of accounting and the application of statistical methods in international business. He is a member of the American Accounting Association, the National Association of Accountants, the Academy of International Business and the Administrative Sciences Association of Canada.